HOW PROFITABLE IS
BIG BUSINESS?

A TWENTIETH CENTURY FUND INVESTIGATION

The Trustees of the Fund approved the program of this survey, underwrote its expenses, and appointed the Special Committee which had charge of it. The Trustees, however, have not assumed responsibility for the findings included in this volume.

HOW PROFITABLE IS
BIG BUSINESS?

*Prepared Under the Direction of the
Corporation Survey Committee of the
Twentieth Century Fund, Inc.*

ALFRED L. BERNHEIM
Editor

ESTELLE SHRIFTE
Assistant Editor

RUFUS S. TUCKER
Director of the Survey

MARGARET GRANT SCHNEIDER
Associate Research Director

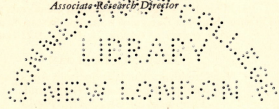

NEW YORK
TWENTIETH CENTURY FUND, INC.
1937

338.7
T918h

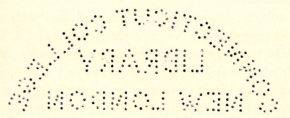

FOREWORD

THIS VOLUME is the second of a series summarizing the results of a study of "big business." The first volume, *Big Business: Its Growth and Its Place,* traced the growth of the corporate form of business organization in the United States, outlined the development of large corporations, and presented a statistical analysis of the distribution of business wealth and income among corporations of various sizes and between corporations as a whole and unincorporated firms.

This book attempts to answer certain questions about the relation between size and profits, size and income and outgo, size and turnover of capital and size and dividends. It contains also an analysis of the profits of groups of specific large American corporations over various periods of time during the present century.

A third volume, now in preparation, will deal with the subject of the compensation paid to corporate officers.

These three books are summaries of certain chapters of a larger study which was made by a special research staff of the Twentieth Century Fund, working under the direction of Rufus S. Tucker. Its object was to find out, as far as the known facts can reveal them, the rôle of the giant corporation in American life. A Special Committee, under the chairmanship of Ralph E. Flanders, has had general charge of the undertaking. The Committee has been asked by the Trustees of the

vii

Fund to make a report, or a series of reports, to the public, on the problems which the research has disclosed, with constructive suggestions for their solution.

The Committee has decided, however, that before it makes its own report, summaries should be prepared and published of the most important parts of the factual material contained in the research reports. Alfred L. Bernheim was asked by the Fund to undertake this task. Mr. Bernheim and his assistants have also revised the original material in the light of data not available when the study was made.

As the reader will see, this book is purely factual. While certain conclusions are drawn from the statistics they also are factual. Economic judgments and suggestions for action have been rigidly excluded. They are for the Special Committee to formulate, and at a later date.

Mr. Bernheim has been assisted by Estelle Shrifte, Assistant Editor, and Sara Lewin, and has had the benefit of the advice and counsel of Frederic Dewhurst, the Fund's economist.

Dr. Tucker was assisted in preparing the original research findings by Margaret Grant Schneider, Associate Research Director of the study. Important contributions were made by Vladimir D. Kazakevitch, and the chapters on banking were originally prepared by C. D. Bremer. Others who assisted in the study were: Clinton Collver, Edward P. Curl, L. V. Farra, M. J. Fields, Samuel E. Gill, Neil E. MacMillan, Betty Malakoff (Secretary), Carolyn H. Stetson, and William C. Willoughby.

Evans Clark, *Executive Director*
Twentieth Century Fund, Inc.

CONTENTS

Contents xiii

APPENDICES

GLOSSARY

ERRATUM

page 165, *line* 3

1919 *should read*, 1909

TABLES

Page

CHARTS

PART ONE

INTRODUCTION

Chapter 1

FINDINGS OF PRECEDING VOLUME
OF SERIES

IN AN earlier publication of the Twentieth Century Fund[1] facts were presented about the structure of American business and the sizes of the units into which it is divided. These will be briefly summarized.

Concentration of Assets in Hands of Giant Corporations

About 57 per cent of all economic activity is incorporated, the range being from 6 per cent in agriculture and related industries to 96 per cent in mining and quarrying. If government is excluded, 62 per cent of all industry is incorporated. Among the more than half-million corporations reporting to the Bureau of Internal Revenue in 1933, there were 594 each of which owned assets of $50 million or over. They numbered only 0.15 per cent of the 388,564 active corporations submitting balance sheets, but they held approximately 53 per cent of the assets of that large group of corporations, of which, numerically, they formed such a minute part.

At the other extreme, there were 211,586 corporations each with assets of less than $50,000. They comprised more than

1. *Big Business: Its Growth and Its Place.*

54 per cent of the total number of corporations but they owned only 1.4 per cent of all corporate assets. Nearly 95 per cent of the total number of corporations had assets of less than $1 million each, but this 95 per cent owned less than 15 per cent of the assets of all corporations. The degree of concentration of corporate wealth in the hands of the giants —corporations with total assets of $50 million and over— varied greatly among branches of industry. It was lowest in construction—2.7 per cent—and highest in transportation and other public utilities, where 1.2 per cent of the corporations owned 83.9 per cent of the wealth.

Concentration of Income[2]

The distribution of the net income of all income-reporting corporations in 1933 also showed high concentration. Sixty-nine corporations, each with a net income of $5 million and over, received about 30 per cent of the net income reported, though they included but 0.06 per cent of all profitable corporations. Nearly three-quarters of all profitable corporations in 1933 had a net income of less than $5,000 each. They accounted for less than 3 per cent of the net income reported.

Of all statutory net income reported, 36 per cent went to corporations with assets of $50 million and over, although these great corporations were only 0.2 per cent of the number of profitable corporations. Forty-seven per cent of all profitable corporations had assets of less than $50,000 each, but

2. Figures on net income cover all reporting corporations. Statutory net income figures cover only active corporations submitting balance sheets. Statutory net income is net income less dividends from domestic corporations and interest on tax-exempt obligations.

this large number of businesses received only 2.2 per cent of the total statutory net income.

When the giant corporations are measured in terms of the total of American economic activity, unincorporated as well as incorporated business, their position, though still conspicuous, loses some of its overpowering prominence. Of the total national income produced, the 594 industrial giants of 1933 accounted for 18.4 per cent; or, if government is excluded, for 20 per cent. The proportion of income produced by giant corporations in the four industrial groups for which figures are separately published in *Statistics of Income*,[3] ranged from 7.4 per cent in trade to 65.5 per cent in transportation and other public utilities.

3. United States Treasury Department, Bureau of Internal Revenue. This source is cited on very many occasions throughout this volume. In order to economize on space, only the title of the publication will hereafter be mentioned.

Chapter 2

THE MEASUREMENT OF PROFITS

THE PURPOSE of this volume is to throw light upon the profitableness, or unprofitableness, of that 57 per cent of American economic activity which is organized in the corporate form—with special attention to the earnings of large as compared with small corporations. It is a subject which has been extensively studied and about which much has been written. Many of the previous studies, however, concern mergers and consolidations rather than large corporations as such. Many of them are confined to the era of trust formation, and few of them cover the years beyond 1929. Some of the more authoritative of the recent studies are briefly summarized in Appendix A.

The subject of corporate profits can be approached from so many different viewpoints and for so many different purposes, that every study is, in a real sense, a new one. Moreover, there is always opportunity for originality in the selection of data, periods covered, and methods of analysis. This book, therefore, is offered as a new approach to the subject.

A. SCOPE OF PRESENT VOLUME

Part One, after briefly reviewing the findings of the preceding volume of the corporation survey series, discusses some of the theoretical aspects of the measurement of profits. The factual material of the present volume is contained in Parts Two and Three, which are related to each other but deal with essentially different aspects of the general subject. Part Four consists of a summary and general conclusions.

Part Two

Part Two analyzes data from *Statistics of Income*[1] which embrace hundreds of thousands of corporations engaged in every type of economic activity and which range in size from the very smallest to the very largest. Only three years—1931, 1932 and 1933—are covered. The figures are aggregates or averages of large numbers of individual items. The size classes and industrial groups into which the corporations are divided do not include absolutely identical corporations in each year.

The emphasis in Part Two is on size in relation to profits, and in relation to other corporate accounting items, such as gross income, total costs, capital structure, turnover of capital, and dividends. Are there differences among classes of corporations of various sizes; are there differences between profitable and unprofitable corporations; are there differences among industries; are there differences between years? These are the questions to which answers are given.

Part Three

The data in Part Three refer to selected, small groups of large, or relatively large, corporations. Various periods of time from 1900 through 1935 are covered. The corporations

1. Except Chapter 9, which is based on data from other sources.

in each group are identical in each year of any stated period under examination. The sources are annual reports of corporations, financial manuals and statistical organizations.

This part shows how profitable leading American corporations have been, studies the fluctuations of their profits over periods of time, and compares profits of different industrial groups. How investors in the securities of large corporations have fared is also considered.

Part Three is a study of "big business" by itself, without any attempt to contrast it with "little business." There is, however, some breakdown of "big" into "big, bigger and biggest."

B. Measurement of Profits

To make profit comparisons significant, absolute profits must first be related to some base. If one corporation has an invested capital of $2 million and another of $1 million, and if each has a net income of $100,000, they are not equally profitable. The larger corporation has earned only 5 per cent on its capital, while the smaller has earned 10 per cent. The smaller is, therefore, twice as profitable as the larger. In other words, rates of profit and not absolute profits must be compared.

There are numerous measures of the rate of profit. None can be singled out as the "true" one. To avoid overelaboration only two measures are employed in the text—the ratio of net income to net worth and the ratio of total profit to total capitalization—but two additional ones are presented in Appendices D and E.

Ratio of Net Income to Net Worth

Net income is what remains when total costs are deducted from gross income. When total costs exceed gross income there is a deficit instead of a net income. In computing the ratios, income taxes are deducted from the net income of the profitable corporations.

Net worth is the sum of the balance-sheet values of all stock issues (preferred and common) and of the surplus and undivided profits.[2] It is often referred to as the "stockholders' equity."

Ratio of Net Income Plus Interest Paid to Total Capitalization

Total profit is net income plus interest paid on borrowed capital. Borrowed capital is usually confined to bonded debt and mortgages, excluding bank loans and other loans not representing investment in the business as a whole, but only incidental to specific transactions.

Total capitalization is net worth plus borrowed capital, thus representing the total investment in the business.

In *Statistics of Income,* however, interest paid is reported as a single sum with no distinction between that paid on bonded debt and mortgages and that paid on notes and accounts. Therefore, when analyzing data from *Statistics of Income,* notes and accounts payable must be added to net worth, bonded debt and mortgages to produce total capitalization. There is some justification for this procedure, since some of the notes and accounts payable may represent investment in

2. Some corporations report deficits instead of surpluses. Where there are deficits, they are deducted from the surpluses to derive the "net surplus."

the business, but whether there is or not, it is unavoidable.

The ratio of total profit to total capitalization is a measure of the productiveness of the entire capital invested in an enterprise. It is a more comprehensive measure than the ratio of net income to net worth, which is a test only of the productiveness of the capital supplied by stockholders.

C. Water In Capital Structure

Much has been said about the presence of "water" in the capital structure of many American corporations. By this is usually meant that the "true" or "fair" value of the assets of a corporation are less than the value placed upon them in its balance sheet—the difference representing the amount of water.

Before the war it was not unusual for promoters to establish a par value for stock much greater than the value of the tangible property behind it. Some of the excess might have been justified as payment for promotional services and allowance for value of patents or good will, but frequently it had no basis at all except the hope of future profits or the desire to deceive investors. Since the war, it has become more usual to issue stock with no par value, which is set up on the corporation's books for less than the amount paid for it by investors. Under this method, if there is any water at all in a newly formed corporation, it is found in the item "paid-in surplus."

The Problem of Measuring Water

No doubt water exists, but how to measure it is the great

problem. What is the true or fair value of assets? Is it their market value; or their original cost (plus appreciation, less depreciation); or their replacement value; or their earning power capitalized? What is market value? Is it the amount a property would bring at a forced sale, or what a competitor is willing to pay to get control of a business? What is replacement value? Is it the cost of exactly reproducing a plant, even though it has become obsolete, or the cost of replacing it with its modern equivalent? At what rate should earnings be capitalized? What is the value of an intangible asset like good will?

These are some of the questions that would have to be answered before the process of valuation could begin. But even if a satisfactory theory of value could be devised—and in any event no one theory could be applied to all forms of business—the job of placing an even approximately accurate valuation on all the corporations of the country could not be done, for it would require an engineering and accounting survey in every case. And if this task could be accomplished, the results would be out of date by the time they were at hand.

Water Disregarded in This Study

For the above reasons, the possible presence of water in the capital structure of corporations must be disregarded. The result may be that comparisons of profits of various size groups are slightly distorted. If, for example, it were a fact that the corporations in the largest size group are watered, while those in the smallest are not, then the comparison of the rates of profit earned by the two groups would not be fair unless allowance were made for the water in the one.

But no one knows whether this is really true. To assume that it is and then to estimate, or guess, the amount of water, might increase the degree of distortion rather than decrease it. It has been proved that there was water in some large corporations when they were formed, but it has been customary for profitable corporations to absorb their initial water by acquiring valuable assets without writing up their capitalization. Furthermore, reinvested profits have gradually displaced water. Finally, the rise in prices of practically all commodities during the World War increased the value of existing assets, so that much of the water previously on the books was automatically eliminated. Assets that had been overvalued became worth the amount at which they had been carried. Moreover, many corporations in the late twenties were generally believed to be intentionally understating their assets. Thus, in dealing with groups of long-established corporations it is unlikely that the amount of water is large enough to result in serious understatement of the rate of profit, or in unsound comparisons between groups.

There is also no reason to suppose that the analysis of stock profits in Chapter 11 would have to be changed if allowance were made for the existence of water. The prices paid for stocks by investors are based upon the opinion of the market, and the market takes account of the reality of the assets, valuing them on the basis of proved or expected earning power without much attention to the figures at which they are carried on the books.

There is a common misapprehension that the mere existence

of water enables a corporation to obtain larger profits. This is obviously impossible. Neither the corporation's customers nor its competitors will permit it to increase the prices it obtains for its products by such a simple bookkeeping trick. A corporation may make its stock look more attractive to uninformed investors by overvaluing it on the books, but it cannot make its products look more attractive to customers by juggling its capital structure. It is true that railroads and other public utilities subject to control by governmental rate-making bodies are entitled by law to a fair rate on their invested capital. It would be a very incompetent rate-making body, however, that would permit a corporation to include water in the amount of capital on which it is entitled to a fair rate of profit.

Stock Dividends and Split-Ups Do Not Create Water

Whatever else may be said about stock dividends and "split-ups," one thing should not be charged against them. These financial devices do not create water in capital structures.

A stock dividend is merely a bookkeeping transfer from the surplus account to the capital account. The number of outstanding shares is increased, the book value of each share is proportionately decreased, and the book value of all the shares is left unchanged. In other words, the stockholders' equity in the business is not increased by a stock dividend.

A split-up does not even involve the capitalization of surplus. All it does is to increase the number of shares that represent the ownership of a given net worth. As in the case of stock dividends, the book value of each share is proportionately reduced, while the aggregate book value is left unchanged.

Neither stock dividends nor split-ups give the stockholders something for nothing, for the value of what they own is not increased by these devices. It may happen—and in boom times it usually does—that stock dividends and split-ups result in a higher valuation of the share capital by the security markets. But that is only temporary. The markets eventually appraise securities on the basis of the assets and earnings applicable to them, the dividends paid on them, and the prospects of future earnings and dividends.

D. Shortcomings of Data in Statistics of Income

The validity of the analysis of data published in *Statistics of Income* is subject to some doubt because in certain important respects these data are defective for the purposes to which they have been applied in this volume. It is impossible to say to what extent more nearly perfect data would bring about modifications of the conclusions that have been reached, but the possibility of some modifications is at least great enough to necessitate a brief exposition of the more serious shortcomings.

Data Cover Three Years Only

The data cover only three years, all of which were years of serious depression. Tabulations embracing a complete business cycle undoubtedly would not only show different results as far as the absolute figures are concerned, but might also change some of the relationships among the assets classes.

Assets Classes of Unequal Range

The nine assets classes used in *Statistics of Income* are exceedingly unequal in the range between their upper and lower limits. The smallest has a range of only $50,000; the largest of about $3 billion.[3] The largest has a range almost sixty times that of the eight other classes combined; the second largest, four times that of the seven smaller classes combined. It is possible that somewhat different relationships might appear with different gradations of assets-size classes. However, the only serious danger of a significant change in the trend would arise from a subdivision of the extreme classes.

Data Do Not Represent Identical Corporations Each Year

Comparisons between one year and another are to some extent weakened by the fact that the data do not cover identical corporations each year. Changes in the make-up of the groups are not great, however, and are due almost entirely to a decrease in the size of unprofitable corporations.

Unequal Distribution of Industrial Groups

Industrial groups are unequally represented within the various assets classes. Consider, by way of illustration, the industrial distribution of the assets of the smallest and of the largest corporations, as shown in Table 1.

Ninety-five per cent of the assets of the giant corporations are in three industrial groups—manufacturing, transportation

3. Theoretically, the upper range of the largest total assets class is infinity, but as a matter of fact the largest corporation in the United States has assets of about $3 billion. (Based on unconsolidated balance sheet.)

TABLE 1

DISTRIBUTION OF ASSETS OF SMALLEST AND LARGEST
CORPORATIONS, BY INDUSTRIAL GROUPS, 1933[a]

Industrial Groups	Percentage Distribution in Each Group	
	Total Assets Under $50,000	Total Assets $50,000,000 and Over
Total manufacturing	20.5	18.5
Transportation and other public utilities	3.0	40.6
Trade	38.4	1.8
Finance	19.5	35.9
Four other branches	18.6	3.2
All branches	100.0	100.0

a. Computed from data in *Statistics of Income for 1933*, pp. 166–167, 173–174, 185–188.

and other public utilities, and finance. But only 43 per cent of the assets of the smallest corporations are in these groups. On the other hand, 38.4 per cent of the assets of the smallest corporations are in trade, while only 1.8 per cent of the assets of the giants are in this branch of economic activity. Consequently when the smallest and the largest corporations are compared, comparisons are being made between groups of businesses that differ from each other not only in size but also in industrial composition. An analysis of the distribution of assets within each industrial group confirms this conclusion.[4] It follows that the influence of size cannot be definitely dis-

4. Twentieth Century Fund, Inc., *Big Business: Its Growth and Its Place*, pp. 60–61.

tinguished from the influence of industrial factors. Therefore, conclusions as to the effects of pure size must be regarded as indicative rather than as final.

Industrial Classifications Too Broad

Classifications in *Statistics of Income* are far too broad to permit precise conclusions as to industrial differences. The *Census of Manufactures* recognizes more than 300 manufacturing industries alone, and even this large number would have to be further subdivided before genuinely homogeneous industries emerged.

Each of the industrial groups in *Statistics of Income* embraces types of businesses whose differences are more significant than are their similarities. A small fleet of taxicabs and a trunk-line railroad are both classified as transportation companies. A pawn broker and an insurance company both come under the head of finance; a hotel and a dyeing and cleaning establishment, under the head of service; a wholesale importing firm and a corner grocery store, under the head of trade.

Primary Data Not Wholly Homogeneous

Finally, it is necessary to bear in mind that the figures published in *Statistics of Income* are compilations of hundreds of thousands of separate income-tax reports, each of which differs as to the care with which it was prepared and as to the accounting system, or lack of system, applied to its preparation. Provisions of the law and Treasury regulations and rulings tend, of course, to bring about a large degree of correspondence, but they still leave room for significant differences. Since the primary data are not wholly homogeneous, an element of uncertainty is introduced. Does a summation multiply the bias of individual reports or does it reduce it because of compensating differences?

Criticisms of Data in Part Three

Detailed criticism of the data in Part Three is not necessary. In some respects they are better than those in Part Two. They extend over longer periods of time and are not confined to a single phase of the business cycle. They cover identical corporations within each group from year to year. As far as industrial classification is concerned, however, they are still far from satisfactory. Furthermore, the compilations in Part Three like those in Part Two, are composites of separate corporate reports which are not homogeneous.

The most important defect of the data in Part Three is that they apply only to the larger corporations, and that they are only small samples of even this small class. When industrial or size classifications are made, the number of corporations in some of the classifications becomes too small to justify much confidence in the validity of industrial or size comparisons. The outstanding advantage of the income-tax statistics, on the other hand, is their extensive coverage.

E. Use of Non-Technical Language

As far as possible, simple and commonly understood words and phrases are used in the text in place of the more technical language of accountancy. For example, where *Statistics of Income* uses "total compiled receipts" and "total statutory

deductions," the text uses "gross income" and "total costs."
The precise meaning of the important words and expressions
that are employed can be found in footnotes and in the
Glossary.

PART TWO

PROFITS OF LARGE VERSUS SMALL
CORPORATIONS

Chapter 3

GROSS INCOME AND TOTAL COSTS

A BUSINESS is profitable if its gross income is larger than its total costs, and is unprofitable if its total costs exceed its gross income. An analysis of income and outgo is, therefore, a necessary first step to a study of the end product—profit or loss on capital.

A. CHANGES IN GROSS INCOME

Table 2 shows that when all corporations are considered, gross income declined between 1931 and 1932 and rose between 1932 and 1933 in each assets class. Since the decline in the first year was greater than the rise in the second, there was in each case a net decline between 1931 and 1933. There are, however, differences among assets classes and between profitable and unprofitable corporations. These are brought out in the table.

Profitable and Unprofitable Corporations Combined

The drop from 1931 to 1932 was very close to 20 per cent for seven of the nine classes. But in the $5 million-to-$10 million class it was only about 12 per cent, while in the giant class it was nearly 24 per cent.

TABLE 2

Changes in Gross Income, by Assets Classes, 1931–1932–1933[a]

(Total Assets Classes in Thousands of Dollars)

Total Assets Classes	Percentage Changes per Corporation in Each Class								
	All Returns			Returns Showing Net Income			Returns Showing No Net Income		
	1931–1932	1932–1933	1931–1933	1931–1932	1932–1933	1931–1933	1931–1932	1932–1933	1931–1933
Under 50	−19.4	4.8	−15.5	− 6.8	28.1	19.4	−17.4	− 8.5	−24.4
50–100	−20.4	9.2	−13.0	− 4.4	32.6	26.8	−19.9	−14.0	−31.1
100–250	−20.5	8.3	−13.9	2.1	29.4	32.0	−22.0	−18.8	−36.7
250–500	−19.7	10.3	−11.4	6.6	30.7	39.4	−22.9	−21.5	−39.5
500–1,000	−21.0	14.1	− 9.8	12.2	29.6	45.4	−28.3	−18.9	−41.9
1,000–5,000	−19.2	12.4	− 9.2	− 0.6	40.0	39.1	−19.6	−23.1	−38.2
5,000–10,000	−12.3	8.3	− 4.9	10.1	13.5	25.0	−16.6	−10.3	−25.2
10,000–50,000	−19.4	8.8	−12.4	− 1.0	17.6	16.4	−22.9	−11.9	−32.1
50,000 and over	−23.7	2.2	−22.0	−10.0	23.5	11.2	−28.7	−18.4	−41.8

a. Computed from data in *Statistics of Income:* 1931, pp. 154–159; 1932, pp. 160–165; 1933, pp. 166–171. Here, and throughout the rest of this volume, unless otherwise noted, data refer to "all active reporting corporations submitting balance sheets."

It should be understood that the percentages in the table show the changes in the averages per corporation in each class, and not the changes in class aggregates. This method of presenting the data was made necessary because the number of corporations in each class changed from year to year. For this reason the measurement of changes in aggregates would give a highly distorted impression of how the different assets classes were affected. As it is, year-to-year changes must be interpreted with reservations, because not only did the number of corporations vary, but the composition of the population in each class also varied. In other words, groups of corporations are not identical in each year. If they were, the percentage changes would differ to some extent from those shown in the table. It is believed, however, that in spite of the shortcomings of the underlying data, the percentages shown give at least a rough idea of the relationship between the assets classes in respect to changes in gross income.

It will be noted that figures for all assets classes combined are not given. The reason for this is too involved and too unimportant to warrant explanation here. It is sufficient to point out that if the same method of measuring change was applied to all classes combined as was applied to the separate classes, the resulting percentages would show grotesque distortions—so grotesque that in several instances the percentage changes for the totals would fall outside the limits of the changes for any of the separate assets classes.

The above discussion applies to all tables in which percentage changes from year to year are measured.

In the upturn of 1933 the best result was had by the $500,000-to-$1,000,000 assets class, a 14 per cent gain; by far the worst, by the $50 million-and-over class, a gain of slightly more than 2 per cent. For the entire period, 1931–1933, the largest assets class had again by far the worst record —an average decline of 22 per cent. The best record was made by the $5 million-to-$10 million class—a drop of only 5 per cent.

Profitable and Unprofitable Corporations Separately

In the profitable group, the largest falling off in gross income between 1931 and 1932—10 per cent—took place in the giant class. Four classes showed increases, the leader being the $500,000-to-$1,000,000 class, with a rise of more than 12 per cent. From 1932 to 1933, each of the nine classes made a gain, with the $50 million-and-over class in seventh position. When the gain is measured from 1931 to 1933, this class is in last position; the $500,000-to-$1,000,000 in first.

Among the money-losing corporations, the greatest drop in gross income between 1931 and 1932 must once more be charged to the biggest corporations, with the $500,000-to-$1,000,000 class a close second. But between 1932 and 1933, four classes did worse than the giants and four did better; while between 1931 and 1933 all but one class showed a smaller falling off than the giants.

Variations Among Industries

Overall figures conceal ever-present industrial variations. Table 3 gives some indication of their extent.

TABLE 3

CHANGES IN GROSS INCOME, BY INDUSTRIAL GROUPS AND BY SMALLEST AND LARGEST ASSETS CLASSES, 1931–1933: ALL CORPORATIONS[a]

Industrial Groups	Percentage Changes per Corporation in Each Class	
	Total Assets Under $50,000	Total Assets $50,000,000 and Over
Total manufacturing	−16.3	−11.5
Chemicals and allied products	−18.9	− 1.2
Metal and its products	−19.6	−16.7
Transportation and other public utilities	1.1	−32.1
Trade	−15.6	−15.7
Finance	−11.4	−19.9

a. Computed from data in *Statistics of Income:* 1931, pp. 161–162, 169–171, 173–175; 1933, pp. 173–174, 181–183, 185–188. Cf. also text in footnote to Table 2.

Table 3 shows the changes for all corporations between 1931 and 1933 for two assets classes only—the smallest and the largest. Four industrial groups and two sub-groups are covered. They are the only ones for which "ungrouped" data are available for the $50 million-and-over assets class.

The gross income decline for corporations in the $50 million-and-over class ranged from about 1 per cent in chemicals to about 32 per cent in transportation and other public utilities. For the under-$50,000 corporations, the range was somewhat smaller—from a rise in gross income of more than 1 per cent in transportation and other public utilities, to a decline of about 20 per cent in metals.

B. CHANGES IN TOTAL COSTS

Changes in total costs from 1931 to 1933 are shown in Table 4.

TABLE 4

CHANGES IN TOTAL COSTS, BY ASSETS CLASSES, 1931–1932–1933[a]

(Total Assets Classes in Thousands of Dollars)

Total Assets Classes	Percentage Changes per Corporation in Each Class								
	All Returns			Returns Showing Net Income			Returns Showing No Net Income		
	1931–1932	1932–1933	1931–1933	1931–1932	1932–1933	1931–1933	1931–1932	1932–1933	1931–1933
Under 50	−16.6	0.9	−15.9	− 6.3	28.9	20.8	−17.1	−10.8	−26.1
50–100	−17.6	4.1	−14.1	− 4.2	33.3	27.7	−18.8	−16.8	−32.5
100–250	−17.9	3.7	−14.8	2.1	29.7	32.5	−20.9	−20.1	−36.8
250–500	−16.9	5.4	−12.4	6.8	31.0	39.9	−21.1	−22.3	−38.6
500–1,000	−17.8	7.8	−11.4	12.6	29.6	45.9	−25.2	−20.5	−40.5
1,000–5,000	−16.0	6.6	−10.4	− 0.6	40.4	39.6	−17.4	−22.8	−36.2
5,000–10,000	− 8.2	3.3	− 5.1	11.6	12.9	26.1	−12.7	−11.7	−22.9
10,000–50,000	−15.6	4.3	−12.0	− 0.4	16.7	16.3	−19.6	−11.5	−28.8
50,000 and over	−21.0	0.8	−20.4	− 8.2	25.9	15.5	−26.2	−19.0	−40.2

a. Computed from data in *Statistics of Income*. See footnote for Table 2 for page references and for a discussion of precautions that must be taken in interpreting year-to-year changes.

Profitable and Unprofitable Corporations Combined

In each assets class, gross costs declined between 1931 and 1932 and between 1931 and 1933, and increased between 1932 and 1933.

In seven classes, the declines from 1931 to 1932 fell within very narrow limits—between 15.6 per cent and 17.9 per cent. In the $5 million-to-$10 million class, however, the decline was only about one-half as large, while in the $50 million-

and-over class it reached a high of 21 per cent.

The increases between 1932 and 1933 ranged from 0.8 per cent to 7.8 per cent. The largest and the smallest assets classes showed almost the same increase—less than 1 per cent. The $500,000-to-$1,000,000 class showed the biggest increase.

Between 1931 and 1933, the smallest reduction in costs was 5.1 per cent in the $5 million-to-$10 million class; the largest, was 20.4 per cent in the giant class. In the remaining classes the reductions ranged from 10.4 per cent to 15.9 per cent.

Profitable and Unprofitable Corporations Separately

In the profitable group, total costs rose between 1931 and 1932 in four assets classes and fell in five. The range was from a rise of 12.6 per cent in the $500,000-to-$1,000,000 class to a drop of 8.2 per cent in the giant class. Between 1932 and 1933 there were large increases in each class—from 12.9 per cent in the $5 million-to-$10 million class to 40.4 per cent in the class immediately smaller. Each class showed an increase also between 1931 and 1933. The largest was 45.9 per cent in the $500,000-to-$1,000,000 class; the smallest, 15.5 per cent in the giant class.

In the unprofitable group, declines occurred throughout. The $500,000-to-$1,000,000 class and the giant class showed, all in all, the highest declines; the $5 million-to-$10 million class, the lowest.

From a comparison of Tables 2 and 4, it can be seen that changes in costs closely paralleled changes in income in each assets class. This is brought out clearly in Chart 1 which shows the changes in the two items between 1931 and 1933.

CHART 1

CHANGES IN GROSS INCOME AND TOTAL COSTS, BY ASSETS CLASSES, 1931–1933

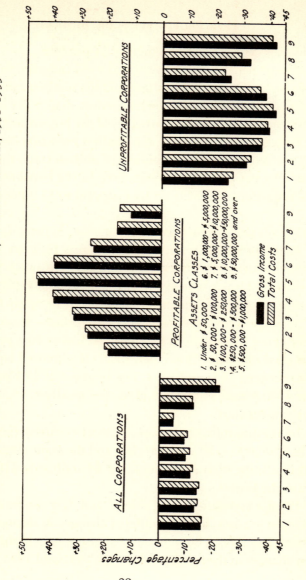

ASSETS CLASSES

1. Under $50,000
2. $50,000 - $100,000
3. $100,000 - $250,000
4. $250,000 - $500,000
5. $500,000 - $1,000,000
6. $1,000,000 - $5,000,000
7. $5,000,000 - $10,000,000
8. $10,000,000 - $50,000,000
9. $50,000,000 and over

Gross Income
Total Costs

ALL CORPORATIONS

PROFITABLE CORPORATIONS

UNPROFITABLE CORPORATIONS

Percentage Changes

Variations Among Industries

Table 5, showing industrial variations for total costs, corresponds to Table 3.

TABLE 5

CHANGES IN TOTAL COSTS, BY INDUSTRIAL GROUPS AND BY
SMALLEST AND LARGEST ASSETS CLASSES, 1931–1933:
ALL CORPORATIONS[a]

| Industrial Groups | Percentage Changes per Corporation in Each Class | |
	Total Assets Under $50,000	Total Assets $50,000,000 and Over
Total manufacturing	−17.3	−11.5
Chemicals and allied products	−19.2	− 0.7
Metal and its products	−21.3	−17.2
Transportation and other public utilities	− 0.7	−28.4
Trade	−16.7	−17.0
Finance	− 5.8	−14.9

a. Computed from data in *Statistics of Income,* page references same as for Table 3. Cf. also text in footnote to Table 2.

In the smallest assets class, transportation and other public utilities showed the smallest decline—0.7 per cent. The largest decline of the major groups was 17.3 per cent in total manufacturing, but both sub-groups under manufacturing showed even larger declines—metal and its products leading with 21.3 per cent.

In the largest assets class, however, the situation was quite different. Here, transportation and other public utilities registered the largest decrease in total costs—28.4 per cent—

while the smallest decrease among the major groups was 11.5 per cent in manufacturing. Chemicals and allied products, a manufacturing sub-group, showed a decrease of less than 1 per cent.

C. RELATIONSHIP BETWEEN GROSS INCOME AND TOTAL COSTS

More important than either income or costs by themselves, is the relationship between them. In Table 6 this is given in terms of percentages of total costs to gross income. All figures above 100 indicate losses, and the further above the greater the rates. Conversely, all figures below 100 indicate profits, and the further below the greater the rates. This is graphically presented for the year 1933 in Chart 2.

TABLE 6
RATIO OF TOTAL COSTS TO GROSS INCOME,
BY ASSETS CLASSES, 1931, 1932 AND 1933[a]

(Total Assets Classes in Thousands of Dollars; Ratios in Percentages)

Total Assets Classes	All Returns			Returns Showing Net Income			Returns Showing No Net Income		
	1931	1932	1933	1931	1932	1933	1931	1932	1933
Under 50	105.9	109.6	105.5	96.3	96.8	97.4	112.8	113.2	110.3
50–100	104.0	107.6	102.6	96.4	96.5	97.0	110.4	111.9	108.2
100–250	103.9	107.4	102.8	95.7	95.8	96.1	111.3	112.9	111.0
250–500	103.5	107.2	102.4	94.7	94.8	95.0	111.7	114.3	113.3
500–1,000	103.6	107.8	101.9	93.7	94.0	94.0	112.0	116.9	114.6
1,000–5,000	103.7	107.8	102.3	92.2	92.2	92.5	114.0	117.1	117.6
5,000–10,000	102.5	107.2	102.3	89.7	90.9	90.5	115.2	120.5	118.6
10,000–50,000	100.3	105.0	100.7	88.9	89.6	88.9	111.6	116.4	117.0
50,000 and over	95.3	98.8	97.3	87.4	89.1	90.8	103.4	107.1	106.3
All corporations	100.5	104.4	100.8	90.9	91.4	92.4	109.5	112.9	111.6

a. Computed from data in *Statistics of Income*, page references same as for Table 2.

CHART 2

Ratio of Total Costs to Gross Income, by Assets Classes, 1933

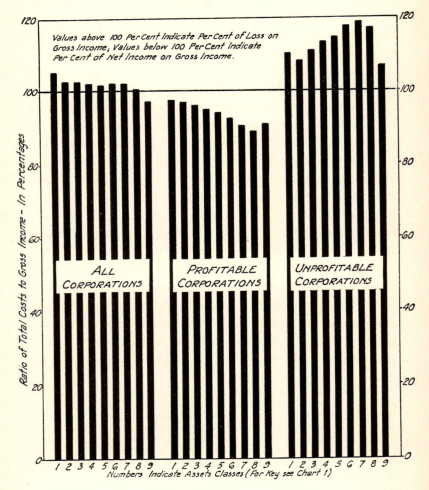

Values above 100 Per Cent Indicate Per Cent of Loss on Gross Income; Values below 100 Per Cent Indicate Per Cent of Net Income on Gross Income.

Ratio of Total Costs to Gross Income — In Percentages

ALL CORPORATIONS

PROFITABLE CORPORATIONS

UNPROFITABLE CORPORATIONS

Numbers Indicate Assets Classes (For Key see Chart 1)

Comparisons Among Assets Classes

In the net income group there is in every year covered a marked tendency for the cost-income ratio to grow more favorable (i.e., declining ratio of total costs to gross income) with increasing size of the assets classes. The only noteworthy exception occurred in 1933, in which year the largest assets class showed a slightly less favorable ratio than either of the two immediately preceding classes.[1]

In the no net income group the trend is not as well defined nor as regular, but is, nevertheless, clear enough to warrant certain conclusions. Beginning with the second smallest class, the ratio grows steadily, though gradually, more unfavorable with increasing size through the $5 million-to-$10 million class. The next larger class, however, exhibits a considerably better ratio, while the $50 million-and-over class shows a further, and very decided, improvement. The giants have by far the best record in all three years.

When all corporations—profitable and unprofitable—are considered, the trend toward a higher percentage of profit on gross income with increasing assets size is, with a few unimportant reversals, steady. The improvement from one class to the next higher is slight until the highest assets class is reached. Here the improvement is decided, especially in 1931

1. If the reader is interested in knowing the per cent of profit or loss on gross income, he need only subtract 100 from the figures shown in the table. Where this difference is a minus quantity, it shows the per cent of profit; where it is a plus quantity, it shows the per cent of loss. To illustrate: under-$50,000 assets class for returns showing net income, 1931: 96.3 minus 100 equals −3.7, or a profit of 3.7 per cent on gross income; under-$50,000 assets class for returns showing no net income, 1931: 112.8 minus 100 equals +12.8, or a loss of 12.8 per cent on gross income.

and 1932.

Comparisons Between Years

Comparisons between years show, with one exception, less favorable ratios in 1932 than in 1931 in all size classes in all groups. The changes were smaller in the net income group than in the no net income group.

For the net income group, however, there were very slightly less favorable ratios in 1933 than in 1932 in six of the nine assets classes, while for the no net income group there were more favorable ratios in 1933 in all but two of the classes. When all returns are considered, the 1933 ratios were more favorable than the 1932 in each assets class.

For all returns, 1933 displayed a slightly better ratio than 1931 in all size classes except the largest two. For the net income group separately, all but one class had a less favorable ratio in 1933 than in 1931, while for the no net income group the ratio was more favorable in 1933 in the smallest three classes and less favorable in the remainder.

Variations Among Industries

In Table 7 the ratios of total costs to gross income are shown for four industrial groups and two sub-groups, for profitable and unprofitable corporations combined in 1933. Only the smallest and largest assets classes are covered.

In the smallest class all groups show costs in excess of gross income, but there are wide differences among them. In trade, costs were only 2.6 per cent greater than income, while, at the other extreme, in finance, costs exceeded income by 26.8

per cent. In the giant class, each group shows an excess of gross income over total costs, but the range is narrow—from 4.4 per cent to 1.5 per cent. Finance, which made the poorest record in the smallest class, made the best in the largest. The chemical group had the poorest results among the giants.

TABLE 7

RATIO OF TOTAL COSTS TO GROSS INCOME, BY INDUSTRIAL GROUPS
AND BY SMALLEST AND LARGEST ASSETS CLASSES, 1933:
ALL CORPORATIONS[a]

(*Ratios in Percentages*)

Industrial Groups	Total Assets Classes	
	Under $50,000	$50,000,000 and Over
Total manufacturing	105.8	97.4
Chemicals and allied products	106.9	98.5
Metal and its products	110.1	98.3
Transportation and other public		
utilities	105.0	96.8
Trade	102.6	96.1
Finance	126.8	95.6

a. Computed from data in *Statistics of Income for 1933*, pp. 173–174, 181–183, 185–188.

Chapter 4

THE RELATIONSHIP BETWEEN SIZE
AND PROFITS BEFORE 1931

STATISTICS OF INCOME is by far the best source for data on the relationship between size and profits. Unfortunately, however, it is of little use for this purpose before 1931, because not until then did the Bureau of Internal Revenue begin the regular publication of income statistics classified by the size of the assets of the reporting corporations. The only earlier data that are usable are a series of figures for the year 1919, and, since 1928, annual tabulations of consolidated returns.

A. RELATIONSHIP BETWEEN SIZE AND PROFITS IN 1919

Statistics of Income for 1919[1] shows that the per cent of net income to invested capital[2] declined almost uninterruptedly from 382.7 per cent on capital under $500 to 9.6 per cent on capital over $100 million. The average for 192,037 corporations of all sizes was 14.1 per cent; the average for the 129 corporations with invested capital of $50 million and over was 9.7 per cent. No class with an invested capital of $20 million or over showed a rate of net income as high as the

1. Pp. 14–17.
2. Invested capital, as used in *Statistics of Income,* is substantially the same as net worth. It does not include borrowed capital.

36

average for all the corporations. The lowest rate—less than 9.2 per cent—was found in the $80 million-to-$90 million class.

Table 8 gives the figures grouped into nine classes to conform with the assets classes used in *Statistics of Income* since 1931.

TABLE 8

RATIO OF NET INCOME TO INVESTED CAPITAL, BY INVESTED CAPITAL CLASSES, 1919[a]

(Invested Capital Classes, Invested Capital and Net Income in Thousands of Dollars; Ratios in Percentages)

Invested Capital Classes	Number of Corporations	Invested Capital (A)	Net Income (B)	Ratio $\left(\frac{B}{A}\right)$
Under 50	114,516	2,157,232	448,315	27.8
50–100	28,295	1,955,091	337,395	17.3
100–250	25,076	3,870,195	670,276	17.3
250–500	10,520	3,664,195	669,580	18.3
500–1,000	6,147	4,292,677	770,334	17.9
1,000–5,000	5,909	12,098,876	2,046,538	16.9
5,000–10,000	785	5,446,057	816,451	15.0
10,000–50,000	660	13,130,879	1,657,819	12.6
50,000 and over	129	19,515,149	1,889,062	9.7
All corporations	192,037	66,130,351	9,305,770	14.1

a. Arranged and computed from data in *Statistics of Income,* 1919, pp. 14–17.

B. CONSOLIDATED RETURNS[3]

Consolidated returns represent businesses which, on the average, are very much larger than non-consolidated enter-

3. ". . . a consolidated return may be filed when one or more chains of

prises. From 1928 through 1933 the average gross income of corporations making consolidated returns was from 38 to 48 times as large as that shown for all returns, exclusive of consolidated;[4] the average net income of those having a net income was from about 20 to 65 times as large; the average deficit of those with deficits was from about 16 to 35 times as large. For these reasons consolidated returns throw at least some light upon the relationship between size and profits.

In 1928 and 1929 less than two-thirds of the corporations filing consolidated returns had any net income; in 1930, less than one-half; in 1931, less than one-third; in 1932, slightly more than one-sixth; in 1933, slightly more than one-fourth. In three of the six years covered, the proportions were a little lower for consolidated returns than for all returns, exclusive of the consolidated.

Consolidated and Non-Consolidated Returns

The average net income of consolidated returns showing net income declined from $830,550 in 1930 to $443,295 in 1933, or 46.6 per cent; but the average net income of all

corporations are connected through stock ownership with a common parent corporation, at least 95 percent of the stock of each of the corporations (except the common parent) being owned directly by one or more of the other corporations, and the common parent corporation owning directly at least 95 per cent of the stock of at least one of the other corporations." *Statistics of Income for 1933*, p. 32.

4. The calculations of the averages of gross and net income and net deficit are based on totals made up of all returns showing net income and all returns showing no net income data, whether or not submitting balance sheets, but leaving out of consideration "returns showing no income data—inactive corporations." There were 57,238 returns in this last named class in 1933.

profitable corporations, exclusive of those using the consolidated form of report, increased 42.1 per cent over the same period, or from $14,037 to $19,949. The average deficit of consolidated returns showing deficits increased from $311,122 in 1930 to $375,976 in 1933, or 20.8 per cent; but the average deficit of all unprofitable corporations, exclusive of the consolidated ones, declined 24.2 per cent, or from $14,185 to $10,759.[5] It may be said that, on the whole, the depression dealt more severely with corporations that filed consolidated returns than with the others.

Consolidated Not Identical with Giant Corporations

While they represent corporations that are relatively large on the average, consolidated returns do not by any means include all of the nation's biggest businesses. For example, in 1932 only about 58 per cent of the corporations with assets of $50 million and over—361 out of 617—made consolidated reports.[6] Since 7,426 consolidated reports were filed in that year, more than 95 per cent must have been filed by relatively small corporations.

Data on consolidated returns have been given because, with the exception of the single series of figures for 1919, they furnish the only information from *Statistics of Income* which has any bearing on size in relation to profits prior to 1931. For the reasons stated in the previous paragraph, however, precise

5. Figures in *Statistics of Income* are given in thousands of dollars. Therefore the averages derived from them are approximations for the three right-hand digits.

6. Twentieth Century Fund, Inc., *Big Business: Its Growth and Its Place*, p. 77.

conclusions as to this relationship should not be drawn. Furthermore, profit ratios corresponding to those given in Chapters 5 and 6 for all corporations cannot be computed for consolidated returns alone, because *Statistics of Income* does not report either the net worth or the total capitalization of this group of corporations.

Chapter 5

NET INCOME ON NET WORTH

FOR THE years from 1931 through 1933, *Statistics of Income* has published comprehensive figures on all reporting corporations, classified by assets size. From these figures two series of profit ratios have been computed. The first—the ratio of net income to net worth[1]—is discussed in this chapter; the second—the ratio of total profit to total capitalization—in Chapter 6.[2]

1. Net income, it should be remembered, is a figure derived by subtracting total costs from gross income. Where the difference is a minus quantity, there is a deficit instead of a net income. In the case of profitable corporations, the income tax has been deducted from net income. For 1933, a small excess profits tax also has been deducted from net income.

Net worth is the sum of the capital stock (preferred and common) and the net surplus and undivided profits.

2. Two adjusted ratios have been computed for the reasons stated below. They are presented in Appendices D and E.

In small corporations, whose stock is usually closely held and whose officers are usually the controlling stockholders, there is a rather tenuous line between profits and officers' compensation. Payments to officers are frequently in rough proportion to their stock holdings, and in part really represent distributions of profits. For this reason, profit ratios for these corporations are heavily affected by managerial policy. As corporations grow larger, as ownership becomes wider, and as the interests of officers and owners become further separated, compensation paid to officers and profits available for dividends become more and more sharply differentiated.

Furthermore, profit ratios were affected by the fact that the depreciation and depletion practices of the larger corporations were less generous than those of the smaller ones in 1931, 1932 and 1933. It is likely that in those years most

41

Table 9 presents the ratios of net income to net worth for three groups of corporations, classified by assets, for the three years ending with 1933. The numerical data from which the computations were made are given in Appendix B.

Profitable and Unprofitable Corporations Combined

Considering, first, the profitable and unprofitable corporations combined, corporations in the largest assets class were the only ones which, as a whole, reported a net income in any of the three years covered. All other classes showed deficits in each year. The deficit ratio was largest, by far, in the smallest assets class, and became progressively smaller as the size of the assets increased. There was no break in the trend in any of the years. To the extent that the ratio of net income to net worth is a true measure of profitableness, bigness was an advantage and smallness a disadvantage, for corporations as a whole, in 1931, 1932 and 1933. These were years characterized by an abnormally severe business depression, and it is impossible to say whether or not this conclusion would be valid for other

corporations made inadequate allowances for depreciation and depletion, and that they therefore overstated their net incomes. Larger corporations made even less adequate allowances than smaller ones and, therefore, overstated their incomes by even larger margins.

Appendix D shows the effect of adding compensation of officers and depreciation and depletion to net income, and Appendix E shows the effect of adding these items to total profit. The purpose of these adjustments is to show what the profit relationships among the assets classes would be if compensation to officers had the same weight in the profit and loss statement of corporations of every size class, and if depreciation and depletion were charged at the same percentages of capital assets in each assets class.

The effect of the adjustments is to place the larger corporations in a much less favorable position in relation to the smaller ones than they occupy in the unadjusted series. Further analysis of this subject will be found in the Appendices.

TABLE 9

RATIO OF NET INCOME TO NET WORTH, BY ASSETS CLASSES,
1931, 1932 and 1933[a]

(*Total Assets Classes in Thousands of Dollars; Ratios in Percentages*)

Total Assets Classes	Year	All Returns[b]	Returns Showing Net Income	Returns Showing No Net Income[b]
Under 50	1931	−21.7	11.6	−52.0
	1932	−33.0	8.7	−46.5
	1933	−21.1	8.6	−37.8
50–100	1931	− 9.1	7.9	−23.1
	1932	−14.0	6.3	−20.8
	1933	− 5.7	6.9	−13.2
100–250	1931	− 6.5	7.0	−17.2
	1932	− 9.9	6.1	−15.5
	1933	− 4.4	6.9	−11.6
250–500	1931	− 4.7	6.8	−13.2
	1932	− 7.4	6.0	−12.5
	1933	− 3.1	7.1	− 9.9
500–1,000	1931	− 3.9	6.6	−10.9
	1932	− 6.4	5.9	−11.1
	1933	− 2.1	7.1	− 8.5
1,000–5,000	1931	− 3.0	6.5	− 8.8
	1932	− 4.8	5.6	− 8.7
	1933	− 1.9	6.7	− 7.5
5,000–10,000	1931	− 1.8	7.0	− 7.6
	1932	− 4.0	5.9	− 8.7
	1933	− 1.7	6.5	− 7.7
10,000–50,000	1931	− 0.5	7.0	− 6.3
	1932	− 2.7	5.9	− 6.8
	1933	− 0.7	6.7	− 6.9
50,000 and over	1931	2.2	7.0	− 1.5
	1932	0.3	5.4	− 2.4
	1933	0.9	4.7	− 2.0
All corporations	1931	− 0.6	7.0	− 6.2
	1932	− 2.8	5.6	− 6.9
	1933	− 0.8	5.7	− 5.7

a. Computed from data in *Statistics of Income*, page references same as for Table 2. For numerical data, see Appendix B.
b. Minus signs indicate deficits.

phases of the business cycle.

Profitable and Unprofitable Corporations Separately

Table 9 brings out also a most interesting divergence in the profit-ratio trend between the profitable and unprofitable corporations. Among corporations with net income, the smallest assets class was the most profitable in each year, while the largest was the least profitable in 1932 and 1933 and only the fourth most profitable in 1931. Among corporations with no net income, the smallest assets class was by far the most unprofitable and the largest was by far the least unprofitable in each year.

Variations Between Years

For all corporations, the deficit ratio was higher in 1932 than in 1931. In the giant class the profit ratio was lower in the later year. In 1933 the deficit ratios were lower than in 1932 in each class, and lower than in 1931 in each class but one. In the giant class, the profit ratio was higher in 1933 than in 1932, but lower than in 1931.

Among money-making corporations, the profit ratios were lower in 1932 than in 1931 in each class. They were higher in 1933 than in 1932 in all but the smallest and the largest classes. In six of the nine classes, the ratios were lower in 1933 than in 1931.

Among money-losing corporations, the deficit ratios were higher in 1932 than in 1931 in four classes, including the largest three, and were lower in five. The 1933 ratios were lower than the 1932 in each class but one, and lower than the

1931 ratios in all except the largest three assets classes.

Variations Among Industries in 1932

The conclusions that have just been stated as to the relationship between size and profitableness can be applied, strictly, only to industry as a whole. As always, variations in the pattern come to light when the overall figures are broken down into different industrial groups.

Tables 10, 11 and 12 show the ratios of net income to net worth for seven important industrial groups and for eleven sub-groups under manufacturing. The computations were based to some extent on special tabulations by the Bureau of Internal Revenue for the Twentieth Century Fund for 1932 only. The ratios can be given, therefore, for that year alone. Furthermore, data were not made available in every instance for each assets class separately, making some gaps in the tables unavoidable.

TABLE 10

RATIO OF NET INCOME TO NET WORTH, BY INDUSTRIAL GROUPS AND BY ASSETS CLASSES, 1932: ALL CORPORATIONS[a]

(Total Assets Classes in Thousands of Dollars; Ratios in Percentages)

Industrial Groups	Total Assets Classes										
	Total	Under 50	50–100	100–250	250–500	500–1,000	1,000–5,000	5,000–10,000	10,000–50,000	50,000 and Over	Classes Grouped[b]
Mining	− 2.8	−53.1	−10.7	− 6.5	− 4.3	− 3.6	− 2.1	− 1.9	− 1.7	− 2.8	—
Total manufacturing	− 3.6	−35.7	−16.3	−11.6	− 8.9	− 6.9	− 5.7	− 4.1	− 4.1	− 0.2	—
Food	0.3	−20.5	− 9.6	− 7.2	− 3.1	− 1.6	− 0.9	− 0.4	− 1.2	4.4	—
Tobacco	13.2	−18.1	− 5.0	− 1.8	− 3.3	− 4.9	3.2	b	b	16.2	7.7
Textiles	− 8.0	−50.3	−21.7	−13.5	− 9.2	− 7.8	− 5.7	− 8.3	b	b	5.3
Leather	− 6.6	−45.4	−20.2	−11.9	−13.4	−10.7	− 7.8	− 8.6	b	b	2.6
Rubber	− 4.2	−37.8	− 7.5	−13.6	− 5.2	−10.8	− 2.5	−	b	b	4.0
Forest products	−10.3	−53.9	−27.0	−19.1	−17.3	−12.4	b	b	− 7.0	− 3.3	8.2
Paper	− 3.4	−28.3	−10.8	− 7.3	− 5.0	− 2.7	− 4.6	− 1.8	b	b	2.8
Printing	− 1.4	−26.3	−13.3	− 6.6	− 2.5	− 1.9	− 0.3	4.7	b	b	0.8
Chemicals	0.4	−25.1	− 9.0	− 5.9	− 2.2	− 0.4	− 1.8	1.2	− 0.1	0.6	—
Stone	− 6.1	−35.2	−15.1	−12.2	−11.1	− 7.7	− 7.1	− 5.6	b	b	2.8
Metal	− 6.4	−40.2	−18.3	−14.5	−12.3	− 9.8	− 9.8	− 7.0	− 7.6	− 3.5	—
Construction	− 7.8	−43.4	−19.2	−13.0	− 9.6	− 6.6	− 1.3	b	b	b	1.7
Transportation & other public utilities	0.7	−19.4	− 8.2	− 3.8	− 2.8	− 6.3	c	− 0.4	1.1	0.9	—
Trade	− 7.2	−30.1	−14.3	−11.3	− 8.6	− 6.7	− 5.3	− 2.1	− 1.3	2.6	—
Service	−10.0	−41.1	−24.7	− 8.8	− 6.2	− 6.9	− 8.6	− 8.9	b	b	− 8.3
Finance	− 3.4	−31.4	− 9.1	− 7.9	− 5.8	− 5.9	− 4.6	− 5.6	− 2.7	0.9	—
All corporations	− 2.8	−33.0	−14.0	− 9.9	− 7.4	− 6.3	− 4.7	− 4.0	− 2.7	0.3	—

a. Based in part on special tabulations made by the Bureau of Internal Revenue for the Twentieth Century Fund. Minus signs indicate deficits.

b. Classes grouped by Bureau of Internal Revenue to conceal data reported and identity of corporations.

c. Less than one-tenth of 1 per cent.

TABLE 11

RATIO OF NET INCOME TO NET WORTH, BY INDUSTRIAL GROUPS AND BY ASSETS CLASSES, 1932: PROFITABLE CORPORATIONS[a]

(Total Assets Classes in Thousands of Dollars; Ratios in Percentages)

Industrial Groups	Total	Total Assets Classes									
		Under 50	50–100	100–250	250–500	500–1,000	1,000–5,000	5,000–10,000	10,000–50,000	50,000 and Over	Classes Grouped[b]
Mining	4.3	25.6	107.1	85.5	70.4	6.5	4.5	3.4	3.9	2.5	—
Total manufacturing	6.0	9.3	7.1	7.0	6.8	6.9	6.7	7.3	6.1	5.4	—
Food	6.8	10.9	7.6	6.7	7.4	8.8	6.4	6.8	6.9	6.5	—
Tobacco	15.1	16.7	4.9	9.2	4.2	2.1	8.7	11.1	12.0	16.2	—
Textiles	4.5	6.3	6.8	6.3	6.5	5.1	4.7	3.6	b	b	3.4
Leather	6.5	7.5	8.9	7.1	7.0	5.8	8.1	5.9	b	b	6.2
Rubber	1.9	15.6	12.5	9.7	5.4	1.6	4.2	—	—	b	0.9
Forest products	5.2	5.8	6.7	5.7	4.1	3.6	b	b	—	—	6.0
Paper	4.3	6.4	6.1	6.7	6.1	6.0	5.4	4.7	b	b	2.1
Printing	5.1	9.7	6.3	7.3	7.2	8.7	7.4	9.5	b	b	2.6
Chemicals	4.9	12.7	7.9	9.5	9.7	10.2	10.4	10.3	5.8	3.7	—
Stone	4.3	7.0	6.1	7.9	5.7	5.1	5.0	5.0	b	b	3.5
Metal	5.5	8.6	7.0	5.8	5.3	5.0	5.0	6.1	7.6	4.7	—
Construction	11.3	12.5	10.7	10.5	10.3	7.9	12.2	b	b	—	13.1
Transportation & other public utilities	4.9	9.2	8.7	8.0	7.7	7.7	6.3	5.1	5.6	4.7	—
Trade	6.8	7.0	5.2	5.2	6.2	6.4	6.0	6.4	7.9	8.1	—
Service	7.1	13.4	8.9	7.9	7.7	6.7	5.3	8.9	b	b	6.8
Finance	6.0	0.7	5.0	4.6	4.4	4.1	4.1	4.9	5.7	10.2	—
All corporations	5.6	8.7	6.3	6.1	6.0	5.9	5.6	5.9	5.9	5.4	—

a. Same as footnote a, Table 10.   b. Same as footnote b, Table 10.

TABLE 12

RATIO OF NET INCOME TO NET WORTH, BY INDUSTRIAL GROUPS AND BY ASSETS CLASSES, 1932: UNPROFITABLE CORPORATIONS[a]

(Total Assets Classes in Thousands of Dollars; Ratios in Percentages)

Industrial Groups	Total	Total Assets Classes									
		Under 50	50–100	100–250	250–500	500–1,000	1,000–5,000	5,000–10,000	10,000–50,000	50,000 and Over	Classes Grouped[b]
Mining	− 4.7	−100.6	−19.4	−11.9	− 9.0	− 7.4	− 4.3	− 3.8	− 3.3	− 3.8	—
Total manufacturing	− 7.6	−46.8	−22.9	−17.3	−14.5	−12.1	−10.0	− 9.1	− 8.3	− 3.0	—
Food	− 8.7	−33.5	−18.1	−14.8	−10.8	− 9.3	− 7.4	− 9.4	− 9.5	—	—
Tobacco	− 5.5	−12.7	−10.0	−12.8	−10.4	−10.7	− 5.6	b	b	—	− 3.6
Textiles	−12.5	−66.3	−30.2	−20.7	−15.5	−13.2	− 9.4	−12.0	b	b	− 8.5
Leather	−15.6	−59.0	−32.9	−20.8	−20.3	−15.5	−12.6	−12.8	− 8.9	—	—
Rubber	− 5.8	−60.0	−14.5	−20.3	−21.6	−17.9	− 5.0	− 7.6	−12.8	− 3.4	—
Forest products	−11.1	−62.6	−31.0	−21.6	−19.6	−14.4	− 9.8	− 7.6	− 7.0	− 3.3	—
Paper	− 5.5	−34.5	−17.9	−12.7	−11.1	− 8.2	− 9.2	− 5.6	− 4.4	− 2.7	—
Printing	−11.3	−34.7	−19.4	−13.9	−10.0	−12.0	− 6.9	− 5.1	− 7.1	—	—
Chemicals	− 2.9	−38.8	−16.2	−13.7	−10.4	− 7.9	− 7.5	− 8.8	− 7.2	− 1.4	—
Stone	− 8.6	−41.2	−18.1	−15.4	−13.0	−11.1	− 9.6	− 7.9	b	b	− 4.8
Metal	− 7.6	−46.9	−22.1	−17.6	−15.7	−12.3	−11.6	− 8.8	− 9.2	− 4.2	—
Construction	−13.4	−52.5	−25.2	−18.5	−16.8	−12.8	− 6.5	− 5.6	—	—	—
Transportation and other public utilities	− 2.9	−41.7	−22.1	−17.0	−15.2	−23.9	− 9.6	− 8.3	− 5.8	− 2.1	—
Trade	−13.9	−39.9	−19.6	−16.0	−13.1	−11.2	−10.2	− 7.8	− 6.1	− 5.3	—
Service	−14.9	−59.9	−38.1	−14.9	−12.2	−12.8	−13.3	−13.4	−13.4	−10.3	—
Finance	− 6.2	−51.7	−15.1	−13.3	−10.2	− 9.7	− 7.5	− 9.6	− 5.8	− 1.0	—
All corporations	− 6.9	−46.5	−20.7	−15.5	−12.5	−11.1	− 8.7	− 8.7	− 6.8	− 2.4	—

a. Same as footnote a, Table 10. b. Same as footnote b, Table 10.

All Corporations by Industrial Groups

Corporations as a whole, profitable and unprofitable together, showed a loss in 1932 (ratio —2.8 per cent). Transportation and other public utilities by themselves, however,
were "in the black" by a narrow margin (ratio +0.7 per cent).
Though manufacturing as a whole showed a loss (ratio —3.6
per cent), two of its sub-groups, food and chemicals, recorded
very small profit ratios, while a third, tobacco, showed a large
one (+13.2 per cent). Of the seven principal industrial
groups, service had the worst ratio (—10 per cent).

In every industrial group and manufacturing sub-group, the
largest deficit ratios were in the smallest assets class. The
range among the principal groups was from —19.4 per cent
for transportation and other public utilities to —53.1 per cent
for mining. Even in tobacco which, as a whole, had a large
net income ratio, there was a deficit ratio of —18.1 per cent
in the under-$50,000 assets class.

Each industrial group and sub-group reported a deficit
ratio for each assets class up to the $1 million-to-$5 million
class. The range within each class is large. Profit ratios appear
first in the $1 million-to-$5 million class, though for all industries combined no assets class, except the $50 million-and-
over, shows a profit ratio.

Among the main industrial groups, the largest assets class
showed a profit ratio of 0.9 per cent in transportation and
other public utilities and in finance, and of 2.6 per cent in
trade. Mining concerns in this class showed a deficit (—2.8
per cent), as did those in total manufacturing (—0.2 per
cent). In construction and in service the two or three largest

assets classes are grouped. Construction showed a net income ratio of 1.7 per cent for all corporations with assets of $5 million and over; service concerns showed a deficit ratio of —8.3 per cent for all $10 million-and-over corporations.

For all corporations in all industries combined there was, as previously stated, an unbroken downward trend of the deficit ratio as assets increased, the largest class actually showing a net income. This, however, was not true of each of the separate groups and sub-groups. For example, in mining the $50 million-and-over corporations not only showed a loss, but a loss larger than that of any of the three other classes with assets of more than $1 million. In service, the least unprofitable class was that with assets of $250,000 to $500,000. The next three higher assets classes were successively more unprofitable. In finance the giant corporations made the best showing, but the $1 million-to-$5 million class did better than the $5 million-to-$10 million class. In manufacturing, the same result was achieved by the $5 million-to-$10 million corporations as by the $10 million-to-$50 million ones.

Profitable Corporations by Industrial Groups

For all the corporations reporting net income in 1932, the smallest assets class showed the highest profit ratio, and the largest assets class showed the lowest. Numerous exceptions are revealed, however, when the overall figures are broken down. The most startling of these occur in trade and in finance. In both these groups the most profitable of the profitable corporations were not the smallest but the largest. In finance the least profitable corporations were the very smallest, while in trade the least profitable were in the second and third smallest classes. Thus profitable corporations in trade and finance showed the reverse relationship between size and profitableness to that shown when all industries are combined. But the unprofitable trade and finance corporations,[3] strange to say, did not deviate from, but followed, the trend displayed by all unprofitable corporations.

Among profitable mining companies, the most profitable class was not the under-$50,000 but the $50,000-to-$100,000 class. This showed the huge net income ratio of 107.1 per cent. Each of the smallest four assets classes among profitable mining corporations showed a profit ratio incomparably higher than that for the corresponding class in any other industrial group or sub-group. But in the next higher assets class ($500,000-to-$1,000,000), the profit ratio of mining corporations dropped precipitously and fell more or less into line with the ratios for this class in the other industrial groups and sub-groups.

In tobacco, the most profitable corporations were the smallest (16.7 per cent ratio), but the largest were almost neck-and-neck (16.2 per cent ratio). The median class, $500,000-to-$1,000,000, had the lowest profit ratio (2.1 per cent). In printing the under-$50,000 assets class and the $5 million-to-$10 million class showed the highest, and virtually the same, profit ratios (9.7 per cent and 9.5 per cent, respectively). Construction's low appeared in the $500,000-to-$1,000,000 class, while under service, the $1 million-to-$5 million class was the least profitable.

3. The next section discusses the unprofitable corporations.

Unprofitable Corporations by Industrial Groups

Among all unprofitable corporations in 1932, the smallest were the most, and the largest were the least, unprofitable. Only three exceptions appear when the total figures are broken down by industries: in mining the smallest deficit ratio is found in the second largest size class; in printing, the $10 million-to-$50 million class[4] showed worse results than the $1 million-to-$5 million or the $5 million-to-$10 million classes; in tobacco the largest deficit ratio was recorded by the $100,000-to-$250,000 class and not by the under-$50,000, but the difference was so small as to be without significance.

The no net income corporations behave in a much more orderly fashion than those reporting net income. In the first place, the separate industrial groups and sub-groups conform more closely to the pattern for all corporations.[5] In the second place, the trend within each group and sub-group is more regular. There are relatively few breaks in the trend of decreasing deficit ratios with increasing size. The most striking of these occurs in transportation and other public utilities where the deficit ratio jumps from −15.2 per cent in the $250,000-to-$500,000 class to −23.9 per cent in the $500,000-to-$1,000,000 class, and then drops sharply to −9.6 per cent in the next larger class. Finance shows a much smaller, but a still noteworthy, break in the trend in the $5 million-to-$10 million class.

The range of deficit ratios was very much wider than that

4. There were no $50 million-and-over corporations reporting no net income in printing in 1932.

5. That is to say all corporations reporting net income, on the one hand, and all corporations reporting no net income, on the other.

of profit ratios. This is true when totals are compared, and for each industrial group and sub-group separately—except mining and tobacco.

Among unprofitable corporations, the largest class in each industry was, with one exception, less unprofitable than the industry as a whole. Among profitable corporations the largest class was less profitable than each industry as a whole—except in trade, finance, tobacco, forest products and construction.

Chapter 6

TOTAL PROFIT ON TOTAL
CAPITALIZATION

A. Profit Ratios

THE PRECEDING chapter analyzed profits earned on stock-holders' equity. This one deals with total profit on total capitalization. It is important to keep in mind that total profit is net income plus interest paid on borrowed capital and that total capitalization is net worth plus borrowed capital.[1] In Table 13 the ratios of total profit to total capitalization are given. The numerical data from which the calculations were made will be found in Appendix C.

The general effect of adding interest paid to net income and borrowed capital to net worth is, with a few exceptions, to narrow the fluctuations from an "even break." Profitable corporations earn slightly smaller rates of profit, and unprofitable corporations incur appreciably smaller rates of loss, than they do when net income is compared with net worth.

When Table 13 is compared with Table 9 it can be seen that the two profit ratios correspond very closely as to the relationship among the assets classes. Some of the more im-

1. Interest includes all interest paid, and borrowed capital includes notes and accounts payable. For explanation of this, see pp. 9–10.

54

TABLE 13

RATIO OF TOTAL PROFIT TO TOTAL CAPITALIZATION, BY ASSETS
CLASSES, 1931, 1932 AND 1933[a]

(*Total Assets Classes in Thousands of Dollars; Ratios in Percentages*)

Total Assets Classes	Year	All Returns[b]	Returns Showing Net Income	Returns Showing No Net Income[b]
Under 50	1931	−10.5	9.2	−22.6
	1932	−15.9	7.2	−21.0
	1933	− 9.6	7.0	−15.6
50–100	1931	− 3.8	6.7	−10.6
	1932	− 6.6	5.8	− 9.7
	1933	− 1.9	6.1	− 5.4
100–250	1931	− 2.2	6.4	− 7.9
	1932	− 4.3	5.8	− 7.0
	1933	− 1.1	6.2	− 4.5
250–500	1931	− 1.0	6.6	− 5.8
	1932	− 2.9	5.8	− 5.6
	1933	− 0.3	6.5	− 3.7
500–1,000	1931	− 0.6	6.5	− 4.7
	1932	− 2.4	5.8	− 5.0
	1933	0.3	6.6	− 3.1
1,000–5,000	1931	− 0.1	6.7	− 3.7
	1932	− 1.5	5.6	− 3.8
	1933	0.3	6.3	− 2.8
5,000–10,000	1931	0.7	7.1	− 2.9
	1932	− 1.0	5.7	− 3.7
	1933	0.5	6.0	− 2.8
10,000–50,000	1931	1.6	6.8	− 2.0
	1932	− 0.1	5.6	− 2.7
	1933	1.1	6.2	− 2.5
50,000 and over	1931	3.6	6.7	1.4
	1932	2.3	5.4	0.8
	1933	2.5	4.7	1.0
All corporations	1931	1.6	6.7	− 1.7
	1932	0.1	5.6	− 2.2
	1933	1.2	5.4	− 1.4

a. Computed from data in *Statistics of Income,* page references same as for
Table 2. For numerical data see Appendix C.
b. Minus signs indicate deficits.

CHART 3

RATIO OF NET INCOME TO NET WORTH AND RATIO OF TOTAL PROFIT TO TOTAL
CAPITALIZATION, BY ASSETS CLASSES, 1933

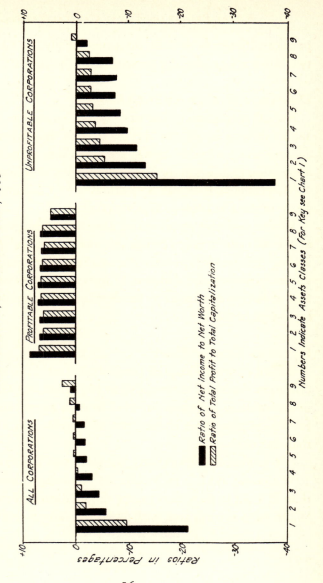

portant differences will be discussed briefly. In Chart 3 the two ratios are graphically presented for the year 1933.

Differences Between the Profit Ratios

For all corporations, the ratio of net income to net worth shows deficits in all but the giant class. But when interest charges and borrowed capital are taken into account, profits appear lower down in the size scale in both 1931 and 1933. In 1931, profits start in the $5 million-to-$10 million class; in 1933, in the $500,000-to-$1,000,000 class.

When profitable corporations alone are considered, neither of the two profit ratios brings out any significant differences among the size groups after the smallest. In the unprofitable group, however, the addition of interest paid to net income and of borrowed capital to net worth results in a profit ratio for the giant class.

Variations Between Years[2]

For all corporations, the ratio of total profit to total capitalization was more unfavorable in 1932 than in 1931 and less unfavorable in 1933 than in 1932 in each assets class. Except for the largest three classes, the 1933 ratio was also better than the 1931.

For profitable corporations, the ratio was less favorable in 1932 than in 1931 in each class, and more favorable in 1933 than in 1932 in each class except the smallest and the largest. When 1933 is compared with 1931, the ratio is less favorable

2. For a discussion of the validity of year-to-year comparisons, see footnote, p. 24.

in the later year in each class except the $500,000-to-$1,000,-
000, but in most of the classes the differences between these
two years are negligible.

For unprofitable corporations, the ratio shows better results in 1932 than in 1931 in each of the smallest four classes,
and poorer results in each of the largest five. Every class
registered an improvement in 1933 over 1932. The ratios were
also less unfavorable in 1933 than in 1931 in all but the largest two classes.

Variations Among Industries in 1932

There are important industrial variations, as a study of
Table 14 will indicate. With the exception of tobacco, all industrial groups and sub-groups[3] showed more favorable, or
less unfavorable, results with the second ratio than with the
first (i.e., Table 14 compared with Table 10). Further analysis
of this table is left to the reader.

B. Variations in Capital Structure

The fact that the profit-ratio relationship among assets
classes changes when consideration is given to interest paid
and borrowed capital, indicates that there must be differences
in the capital structure of the corporations in the various
classes. Table 15 proves that this is so.

The two left-hand columns under each of the three groups
of returns show the relationship between the stockholders'
equity (net worth) and the creditors' claims (borrowed
capital). It is clear that the percentage of borrowed capital

---

3. All assets classes combined in each group and sub-group.

TABLE 14

RATIO OF TOTAL PROFIT TO TOTAL CAPITALIZATION, BY INDUSTRIAL GROUPS AND BY ASSETS CLASSES, 1932: ALL CORPORATIONS[a]

(Total Assets Classes in Thousands of Dollars; Ratios in Percentages)

Industrial Groups	Total	Under 50	50–100	100–250	250–500	500–1,000	1,000–5,000	5,000–10,000	10,000–50,000	50,000 and Over	Classes Grouped[b]
Mining	− 1.3	−17.8	− 6.2	− 3.6	− 1.8	− 2.2	− 0.9	− 7.3	− 0.6	− 1.3	—
Total manufacturing	− 1.9	−19.3	− 9.6	− 7.1	− 5.7	− 4.5	− 3.8	− 2.4	− 2.6	0.9	—
Food	1.3	−10.7	− 4.9	− 3.6	− 1.1	− 1.3	0.3	0.8	c	5.1	—
Tobacco	11.1	−12.4	− 2.6	− 0.5	− 1.4	− 3.4	3.2	b	b	6.8	15.4
Textiles	− 5.8	−26.5	−12.9	− 7.8	− 6.1	− 5.3	− 4.0	− 6.1	b	b	− 4.3
Leather	− 4.7	−25.3	−12.0	− 7.4	− 9.3	− 7.6	− 5.7	− 6.0	b	b	− 2.6
Rubber	− 1.1	−15.5	− 3.8	− 8.4	− 2.9	− 8.2	− 1.1	—	b	b	− 0.7
Forest products	− 6.7	−26.3	−14.5	−11.9	−12.2	− 8.3	b	b	− 5.3	− 4.2	− 1.7
Paper	− 1.1	−15.6	− 6.3	− 4.3	− 2.9	− 1.3	− 2.6	− 0.4	b	b	− 1.7
Printing	0.1	−14.3	− 8.2	− 3.7	− 0.9	− 0.2	0.8	4.9	b	b	1.5
Chemicals	1.4	−13.1	− 5.0	− 3.4	− 0.8	0.5	2.2	1.9	0.6	2.5	—
Stone	− 4.0	−19.4	− 9.3	− 7.6	− 7.4	− 5.2	− 4.6	− 3.6	b	b	1.8
Metal	− 4.6	−21.9	− 5.7	− 9.6	− 8.6	− 7.0	− 7.5	− 5.1	− 5.6	− 2.3	—
Construction	− 3.0	−20.7	− 9.9	− 6.7	− 4.6	− 3.0	0.1	b	b	b	3.8
Transportation and other public utilities	2.7	− 9.5	− 3.7	− 0.8	− 0.1	− 1.7	2.0	1.5	2.8	2.9	—
Trade	− 3.9	−15.7	− 8.2	− 6.4	− 5.0	− 3.7	− 2.9	− 0.7	− 0.4	0.9	—
Service	− 3.6	−17.6	− 6.5	− 2.3	− 0.7	− 0.5	− 1.0	− 2.6	b	b	− 2.3
Finance	− 0.8	−12.4	− 2.2	− 1.3	− 0.4	− 0.5	− 0.1	− 0.9	0.9	4.0	—
All corporations	− 0.1	−15.9	− 6.6	− 4.3	− 2.9	− 2.4	− 1.5	− 1.0	− 0.1	2.3	—

a. Same as footnote a, Table 10.   b. Same as footnote b, Table 10.   c. Less than one tenth of 1 per cent.

59

TABLE 15

DISTRIBUTION OF TOTAL CAPITALIZATION AND OF BORROWED CAPITAL, BY ASSETS CLASSES, 1933[a]

Percentage Distribution

Total Assets Classes	All Returns				Returns Showing Net Income				Returns Showing No Net Income			
	Total Capitalization		Borrowed Capital		Total Capitalization		Borrowed Capital		Total Capitalization		Borrowed Capital	
(*Thousands of Dollars*)	Net Worth	Borrowed	Fixed	Floating	Net Worth	Borrowed	Fixed	Floating	Net Worth	Borrowed	Fixed	Floating
Under 50	51.9	48.1	21.6	78.4	70.1	29.9	13.3	86.7	45.4	54.6	23.3	76.7
50–100	59.3	40.7	35.6	64.4	72.3	27.7	21.1	78.9	53.5	46.5	39.4	60.6
100–250	60.4	39.6	44.2	55.8	73.7	26.3	26.5	73.5	54.2	45.8	49.0	51.0
250–500	63.6	36.4	50.0	50.0	76.3	23.7	31.1	68.9	57.2	42.8	55.2	44.8
500–1,000	66.5	33.5	53.5	46.5	78.8	21.2	36.4	63.6	59.9	40.1	58.3	41.7
1,000–5,000	69.9	30.1	58.1	41.9	79.3	20.7	43.5	56.5	64.9	35.1	62.8	37.2
5,000–10,000	69.9	30.1	65.7	34.3	79.8	20.2	55.3	44.7	64.0	36.0	69.1	30.9
10,000–50,000	69.7	30.3	72.1	27.9	76.5	23.5	67.1	32.9	64.9	35.1	74.5	25.5
50,000 and over	65.1	34.9	82.7	17.3	71.0	29.0	75.3	24.7	61.3	38.7	86.4	13.6
All corporations	66.2	33.8	70.3	29.7	74.0	26.0	63.9	36.1	61.4	38.6	72.9	27.1

a. Computed from data in *Statistics of Income for 1933*, pp. 166–171. Note that "Total Capitalization" covers common and preferred stock and surplus and undivided profits under "Net Worth," and bonded debt and mortgages plus notes and accounts payable, under "Borrowed." The bonded debt and mortgages constitute the "Fixed" part of "Borrowed Capital"; notes and accounts payable constitute the "Floating" part.

Data are given for 1933 only. The trends in the other two years correspond very closely to that of 1933.

to total capitalization tends to decrease with increasing size. The giant corporations show a reversal of this trend, but, on the whole, the corporations with assets of more than $500,000 get a greater proportion of their capital from stockholders and a smaller proportion from lenders than do the smaller ones. On this score the larger corporations are "safer" than the smaller ones. Class for class, the profitable corporations owe less money in relation to their total capitalization than do the unprofitable ones. As size increases, the difference between the profitable and unprofitable groups tends to narrow.

The two right-hand columns show the relationship between "fixed" debt (bonded debt and mortgages) and "floating" debt (notes and accounts payable). There is a striking tendency for the proportion of fixed debt to increase with increasing assets size. Since bonds and mortgages have fixed maturity dates while notes and accounts payable are subject to call by creditors, the larger corporations, again, have greater safety than the smaller ones. They are therefore often able to avoid receivership during a depression while the smaller concerns, even with similar changes in gross business and profit margins per unit of output, often are not.[4]

4. It is, of course, true that every so-called "fixed," long-term obligation eventually matures and must be paid off if it cannot be renewed or refunded. It is also true that not all bank loans are subject to call. Some proportion of them is in the form of time loans, but the time seldom extends more than six months, and usually not more than ninety days; in other words not long enough to carry a corporation from bad business back to good. Accounts payable, which essentially are short-term loans, generally are due in thirty or sixty days. Bank and merchandise creditors, particularly the latter, usually "carry" their debtors for some period of time before instituting bankruptcy proceedings, especially if the debtors' difficulties seem to them to be of a temporary nature.

In spite of these exceptions, however, the generalizations expressed in the

It is interesting, however, that, class for class, the floating debt reported by profitable corporations is a larger proportion of their total debt than that reported by unprofitable corporations. This may be explained on the plausible assumption that the unprofitable corporations find it difficult to obtain bank and merchandise credit, especially during years of business depression.

Chart 4 illustrates the differences in capital structure among assets classes for all corporations.

text hold good. A relatively large volume of bank loans and accounts payable constitutes a greater source of danger than do relatively large issues of bonds and mortgages.

CHART 4

Composition of Capital Structure, by Assets Classes, 1933

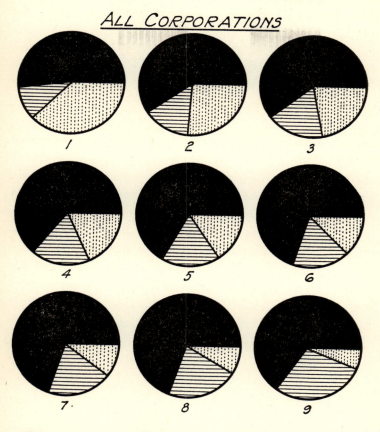

ALL CORPORATIONS

● Net Worth   ⊖ Fixed Debt   ⊛ Floating Debt
Numbers Indicate Assets Classes
(For Key see Chart 1)

Chapter 7

THE INFLUENCE OF TURNOVER ON
RATE OF PROFIT

THE DIFFERENCE between gross income and total costs (i.e., the net income or deficit) determines the profit or loss on sales and other operations. But the rate of profit or loss on capital is not known until the net income or deficit is related to the capital invested in an enterprise, as was done in Chapters 5 and 6. To illustrate, a net income of $100,000 may cover only a small fraction of the stipulated dividend on the preferred stock of one corporation, while it may equal a large percentage on the common stock of another. A loss of like amount may plunge one corporation into bankruptcy, while it may make only a slight dent in the surplus of another. With any given amount of net income or deficit, the larger the capital the smaller the rate of profit or loss on that capital; conversely, the smaller the capital the larger the rate.

The Link Between Net Income or Deficit and the Rate of
   Profit or Loss
   The "turnover" of capital in relation to net income or deficit determines the rate of profit or loss on capital. Turnover is

the ratio of gross income[1] to capital. If the gross income is exactly equal to the capital, however defined, the turnover is one; or, expressed as a percentage, it is 100. In such case the ratio of net income or deficit to gross income is the same as the rate of profit on capital. If the gross income is larger than the capital, the turnover is larger than one, or 100 per cent; if the gross income is smaller than the capital, the turnover is smaller than one, or 100 per cent. In the former case, the rate of profit or deficit on capital is larger than the rate of profit or deficit on gross income; in the latter, the rate of profit or deficit on capital is smaller than the rate of profit or deficit on gross income.

Hypothetical Illustration

If a corporation in one year had a capital of $100,000, gross income of $100,000 and total costs of $90,000, its turnover would be 100 per cent, its dollar net income, $10,000, its rate of net income on gross income 10 per cent, and its rate of profit on capital, 10 per cent.

Assume that in the following year this corporation still had a capital of $100,000 but that its gross income had risen to $150,000 and its total costs to $135,000.[2] This would repre-

---

1. Frequently, probably more often than otherwise, turnover is the ratio of sales, and other income from operations, to capital. In other words income not arising out of the principal activity of a business is excluded, such as dividends and interest on investments (in the case of a non-financial corporation), rents, and profits on the sale of capital assets. For some purposes this is the more appropriate definition of turnover. The wider definition is, however, more pertinent to the discussion in this volume, which is concerned with net profit resulting after all costs (cash and bookkeeping) are deducted from income from all sources.

2. Actually, costs would in all likelihood not rise in the same proportion

sent an increase in turnover from 100 per cent to 150 per cent and an increase in dollar net income from $10,000 to $15,000. The rate of net income on gross income would, however, still be 10 per cent, but the rate of profit on capital would now be 15 per cent instead of 10 per cent.

In the third year this $100,000 corporation had, it is assumed, a gross income of $90,000, total costs of $81,000[3] and a dollar net income of $9,000. This would mean a turnover of 90 per cent, a rate of net income on gross income of 10 per cent, as before, but a rate of profit on capital of only 9 per cent.[4]

Relationship Between Size and Turnover

Table 16 shows the turnover of total capitalization and of net worth for groups of corporations classified by assets,[5] and Chart 5 illustrates the data for total capitalization for the year 1933.

The figures in Table 16 make it clear that turnover de-

---

as gross income, but in order not to complicate the exposition and to bring out the principle in the clearest manner, the assumption throughout is that changes on both sides of the income statement are of equal percentage.

3. Again to avoid the introduction of a complicating factor, it is assumed that total costs declined in the same proportion as the decline in gross income.

4. A corresponding hypothetical illustration could be given for a corporation incurring a deficit.

5. Classification by size of capital would be more appropriate, but the nature of the basic data does not permit this. However, when the average capital (net worth or total capitalization) per corporation is computed for each assets class, it is found that the average size of capital increases with increases in average size of assets. Therefore conclusions based on Table 16 are undoubtedly valid, and, for the purpose at hand, it is proper to look upon the relationship of the assets classes, in respect to turnover, as representing, roughly, the relationship between capital classes in this respect.

CHART 5

TURNOVER OF TOTAL CAPITALIZATION, BY ASSETS CLASSES, 1933

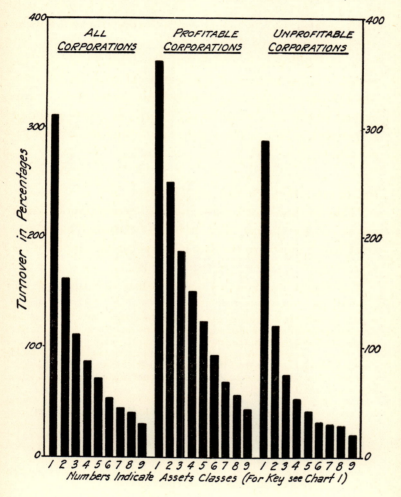

ALL CORPORATIONS · PROFITABLE CORPORATIONS · UNPROFITABLE CORPORATIONS

Turnover in Percentages

Numbers Indicate Assets Classes (For Key see Chart 1)

TABLE 16

TURNOVER OF TOTAL CAPITALIZATION AND OF NET WORTH, BY ASSETS CLASSES, 1931, 1932 AND 1933[a]

(Total Assets Classes in Thousands of Dollars; Turnover in Percentages)

Total Assets Classes	Total Capitalization or Net Worth	All Returns			Returns Showing Net Income			Returns Showing No Net Income		
		1931	1932	1933	1931	1932	1933	1931	1932	1933
Under 50	T. C.	317.1	288.6	310.9	289.2	282.9	360.8	340.5	290.2	287.8
	N. W.	364.0	341.3	373.0	318.5	304.8	381.3	405.4	353.1	368.4
50–100	T. C.	185.0	146.0	161.2	194.8	181.5	249.0	177.4	135.7	119.1
	N. W.	224.6	180.9	200.6	228.1	202.0	269.1	221.7	173.9	159.8
100–250	T. C.	129.9	102.1	111.3	145.7	142.6	186.1	118.2	90.0	74.6
	N. W.	163.2	131.3	143.6	176.7	163.0	203.7	152.5	120.2	105.4
250–500	T. C.	98.7	77.8	86.4	117.0	115.6	151.0	86.2	65.4	52.7
	N. W.	125.3	99.7	111.1	141.3	132.1	165.6	113.3	87.4	74.6
500–1,000	T. C.	80.2	62.2	70.8	96.2	98.4	123.6	70.2	50.0	41.9
	N. W.	100.7	78.9	90.0	115.1	112.7	135.7	90.9	65.7	58.2
1,000–5,000	T. C.	59.8	47.1	53.2	77.7	68.9	92.3	49.6	39.6	32.0
	N. W.	73.9	58.7	66.5	91.4	80.3	102.8	63.1	50.5	42.8
5,000–10,000	T. C.	47.7	40.5	44.3	64.0	61.7	68.1	38.1	31.7	29.9
	N. W.	60.3	52.1	56.8	75.7	72.7	77.6	50.1	42.3	41.5
10,000–50,000	T. C.	47.2	37.2	40.3	56.1	50.6	56.5	40.7	31.1	28.8
	N. W.	60.6	48.6	52.9	69.2	63.3	68.1	53.9	41.5	40.4
50,000 and over	T. C.	36.6	28.9	29.5	45.6	41.2	43.4	30.5	23.0	20.5
	N. W.	52.0	41.5	42.5	60.8	54.6	56.8	45.3	34.4	31.7
All corporations	T. C.	55.0	44.1	47.4	66.4	58.0	69.9	47.4	38.1	33.5
	N. W.	73.5	59.7	64.4	84.0	73.1	85.5	65.7	53.3	48.8

a. Computed from data in Statistics of Income, page references same as for Table 2. Turnover is the ratio of gross income to either total capitalization or net worth.

creased steadily with increasing assets size, and therefore also with increasing capital size.[6] This was so in all three years and in each of the three groups, with a few insignificant exceptions. With the exception of the smallest class in 1931 and 1932 the turnover of capital of the profitable corporations was greater than that of the unprofitable—class for class and year for year.

For all assets classes combined, the turnover in 1932 was lower than in 1931 for each of the three groups. Comparing 1933 with 1932, the turnover was higher in the later year for profitable concerns, and also for profitable and unprofitable concerns combined. But when only the unprofitable concerns are considered, the 1933 turnover was at a still lower rate than the 1932. Nineteen thirty-three showed a higher turnover than 1931 in the profitable group only.

Variations Among Industries

Table 17 contains the figures on turnover in 1933 in the four industrial groups and the two manufacturing sub-groups for which ungrouped data are available for each assets class. It shows that there are wide differences among the groups. At the extremes are trade and finance—the former with a very large, and the latter with a very small, turnover.[7] The widest range[8] within any one group occurs in trade; the narrowest, in finance.

6. See footnote 5, p. 66.
7. In the giant class, however, transportation showed a lower turnover of total capitalization than finance.
8. Measured in points.

TABLE 17

Turnover of Total Capitalization and of Net Worth, by Industrial Groups and by Assets Classes, 1933: All Corporations[a]

(Total Assets Classes in Thousands of Dollars; Turnover in Percentages)

Total Assets Classes	Total Capitalization or Net Worth	Manufacturing			Transportation and Other Public Utilities	Trade	Finance
		Total	Chemicals	Metal			
Under 50	T. C.	327.1	238.6	206.2	243.0	460.8	65.2
	N. W.	361.5	261.8	231.6	296.6	494.7	106.4
50–100	T. C.	200.2	169.4	120.9	122.8	295.7	33.5
	N. W.	220.2	182.7	135.1	148.4	320.6	54.7
100–250	T. C.	150.4	141.9	92.1	74.4	242.9	21.3
	N. W.	164.9	151.4	100.9	95.0	266.4	35.9
250–500	T. C.	118.7	113.0	81.1	52.0	217.1	20.1
	N. W.	128.7	119.2	87.7	74.6	236.9	31.9
500–1,000	T. C.	102.3	108.2	70.9	36.9	189.7	22.3
	N. W.	111.3	115.1	76.9	53.1	206.5	32.9
1,000–5,000	T. C.	80.6	88.0	58.7	23.9	185.4	15.5
	N. W.	87.9	93.9	63.7	39.4	203.9	20.8
5,000–10,000	T. C.	67.3	87.5	55.2	18.5	169.8	16.0
	N. W.	76.0	95.8	61.8	31.1	185.5	21.2
10,000–50,000	T. C.	59.5	71.2	43.3	18.6	150.2	17.7
	N. W.	66.6	77.5	48.3	34.5	180.3	22.8
50,000 and over	T. C.	55.6	46.3	43.4	14.9	156.1	24.8
	N. W.	62.7	51.4	48.5	26.8	179.7	25.2
All corporations	T. C.	72.3	56.5	50.4	16.5	214.8	20.0
	N. W.	80.6	62.3	56.0	29.6	239.3	26.1

a. Computed from data in *Statistics of Income for 1933,* page references same as for Table 7.

With the exception of finance, the general direction of the turnover trend in each industrial group is the same as that for all industries—namely decreasing turnover with increasing size. In finance there is no downward trend after the fourth smallest class. In fact, beginning with the sixth class, the trend is mildly upward.

Turnover an Explanation of Relationship Between Size and Rate of Profit

When the ratio of net income to net worth was computed,[9] the results showed that among profitable corporations the rate of profit decreased as the size classes increased, and that among unprofitable corporations the rate of loss decreased with increasing assets. There were only a few unimportant breaks in these trends. To put it in another way, the smallest corporations showed the largest ratios of profit or deficit, while the largest corporations showed the smallest profit or deficit ratios.[10] The range of the fluctuation from an "even break" was greatest for the smallest corporations and narrowed steadily with increasing assets size.

What, then, is there inherent in size which produces the above relationships? Why should the largest corporations be the least profitable among the profitable and the least unprofitable among the unprofitable; the smallest, the most profitable among the profitable and the most unprofitable among the unprofitable?

9. Chapter 5.
10. Except in 1931 when the $1 million-to-$5 million class showed the smallest rate of profit among the profitable corporations.

If with increasing size there were a tendency toward a decreasing percentage of net income on gross income (or a decreasing percentage of loss on gross income), this might be an adequate explanation. But Table 7 proves that, for profitable corporations, the per cent of net income on gross income, rose steadily with increasing assets size, with the only important break occurring in one year in the largest assets class. This class, nevertheless, even in that year recorded a better ratio than any other except the two immediately smaller —both of which consist of large corporations. For returns showing no net income, the trend was very irregular.

On the whole, the data strongly support the thesis that the trend of the ratio of net income to gross income runs generally counter to the trend of the rate of profit on capital—both being related to variations in size.

Turnover must be looked to for an explanation of this relationship. As already pointed out,[11] the ratio of net income (or loss) to gross income is translated into greater or lesser ratios of profit (or loss) on capital, as the turnover exceeds or falls short of 100 per cent.[12] As there is a very marked trend for turnover to decrease with increasing size, a group of corporations with average capital of a certain size may show a larger net income (or deficit) on gross income than another group with a smaller average capital; yet the larger capital-size group, because of smaller turnover, may show a smaller rate of profit (or deficit) on capital than the smaller capital-size group.

11. See pp. 64–66.
12. I.e., the point at which gross income and capital are exactly even.

Chapter 8

DIVIDENDS

THE PURPOSE of this chapter is to discover whether there is any relationship between the size of corporations and the dividends they pay. Changes in dividends from year to year are first discussed. Then the ratio of dividends to profits is analyzed. Finally there is an analysis of the ratio of total dividends to net worth and of common dividends to common stock.

A. CHANGES IN DIVIDEND PAYMENTS

Changes in total cash dividend[1] payments are shown in Table 18.

Profitable and Unprofitable Corporations Combined

There is no definite dividend-change trend among the assets classes. Certain facts, however, stand out. On the whole, the smallest five classes reduced dividend payments by larger percentages than the largest four. There is only one instance of an increased payment—in the $10 million-to-$50 million

1. Throughout this chapter, dividends should be understood to mean dividends paid in cash. Dividends paid in stock are not discussed because of their unimportance during the period covered. In 1933, for instance, stock dividends amounted to less than 3 per cent of cash dividends.

TABLE 18

Changes in Dividends, by Assets Classes, 1931–1932–1933[a]

(*Total Assets Classes in Thousands of Dollars*)

Total Assets Classes	Percentage Changes per Corporation in Each Class								
	All Returns			Returns Showing Net Income			Returns Showing No Net Income		
	1931–1932	1932–1933	1931–1933	1931–1932	1932–1933	1931–1933	1931–1932	1932–1933	1931–1933
Under 50	−46.2	− 5.2	−49.0	+ 3.2	−39.7	−37.8	−46.8	+20.7	−35.8
50–100	−34.3	−10.6	−41.2	+13.4	−46.4	−39.2	−32.7	+22.4	−17.6
100–250	−37.1	−19.8	−49.5	+ 7.7	−33.2	−28.0	−39.8	−41.7	−64.9
250–500	−33.5	−23.9	−49.4	+ 5.7	−33.3	−29.5	−35.7	−48.5	−66.9
500–1,000	−30.7	−16.5	−42.1	+ 3.4	−24.0	−21.4	−32.1	−45.2	−62.8
1,000–5,000	−29.6	−12.2	−38.2	− 2.0	−11.8	−13.6	−30.1	−45.8	−62.1
5,000–10,000	−29.9	−12.6	−38.7	− 2.8	−18.7	−21.0	−38.6	−30.4	−57.2
10,000–50,000	−26.4	+ 2.3	−24.8	− 4.6	+ 4.9	+ 0.1	−25.4	−38.8	−54.4
50,000 and over	−36.5	−22.4	−50.7	−19.8	− 3.0	−22.2	−43.6	−54.2	−74.2

a. Computed from data in *Statistics of Income,* page references same as for Table 2. Cf. also text in footnote to Table 2.

class between 1932 and 1933. This class, furthermore, made the least reduction between 1931 and 1932, and between 1931 and 1933. The smallest class made the largest reduction between 1931 and 1932, and close to the largest reduction between 1931 and 1933. But of the eight classes that reduced dividends in 1933, its percentage was the smallest. Only two classes cut dividend payments in 1932 more than the giants, and only one cut them more in 1933. Between 1931 and 1933, the giants made the very largest reduction.

Profitable Corporations

Among profitable corporations there is a clear trend—after

the second smallest class—for dividend changes between 1931 and 1932 to become increasingly less favorable with increasing assets size. The smallest five classes show increases; the largest four, decreases. The 1932–1933 changes reveal the opposite trend—with some breaks, however. In general, the changes become less unfavorable with increasing size. The sub-giant class is the only one showing an increase between these two years. No trend is discernible between 1931 and 1933.

The worst showing between 1931 and 1932 was made by the giant class; between 1932 and 1933 and between 1931 and 1933, by the second smallest class. The second smallest class made the best showing between 1931 and 1932; the sub-giants, the best for the two other year-to-year comparisons.

Unprofitable Corporations

Among unprofitable corporations there is again no trend among the assets classes between any two years. The smallest class had the poorest results when dividend changes between 1931 and 1932 are measured, but the giant class was a close second. The sub-giants had the best results. Between 1932 and 1933 the smallest two classes increased their dividends by more than a fifth. All other classes made substantial reductions, the giants having made the largest. All classes lowered dividends between 1931 and 1933. The second smallest class made the smallest reduction; the giant class made the largest.

Class for class and year for year, the unprofitable corporations took less favorable dividend action than the profitable. There were, however, four exceptions. Each of the smallest two classes in the unprofitable group increased their dividend payments in 1933 over 1932, while the profitable corporations in these classes decreased them. These two classes in both groups paid lower dividends in 1933 than in 1931, but the falling off was greater for the profitable than for the unprofitable group.

Variations Among Industries

Examples of variations among industries are brought out in Table 19.

TABLE 19

CHANGES IN DIVIDENDS, BY INDUSTRIAL GROUPS AND BY SMALLEST AND LARGEST ASSETS CLASSES, 1931–1933: ALL CORPORATIONS[a]

Industrial Groups	Percentage Changes per Corporation in Each Class	
	Total Assets Under $50,000	Total Assets $50,000,000 and Over
Total manufacturing	−57.2	−48.2
Chemicals and allied products	−58.7	−50.8
Metal and its products	−70.0	−59.6
Transportation and other public utilities	−47.1	−50.3
Trade	−24.9	−48.2
Finance	−58.6	−56.7

a. Computed from data in *Statistics of Income:* 1931, pp. 160–161, 168, 170–171, 173–175; 1933, pp. 173–174, 181–183, 185–188. Cf. text in footnote to Table 2.

All the industries covered cut dividends between 1931 and 1933, both in the smallest and in the largest assets classes. The range in the largest class, is, however, very narrow—from a reduction of 48.2 per cent in total manufacturing and in trade to one of 59.6 per cent in metal and its products. In the smallest class the range was much wider—from 24.9 per cent in trade to 70 per cent in metals.

B. RATIO OF DIVIDENDS TO PROFITS

The percentage of net income paid in dividends[2] by profitable corporations during 1931, 1932 and 1933 increased as the assets classes increased, as can be seen in Table 20.

TABLE 20

RATIO OF DIVIDENDS TO NET INCOME, BY ASSETS CLASSES, 1931, 1932 AND 1933: PROFITABLE CORPORATIONS[a]

(*Total Assets Classes in Thousands of Dollars; Ratios in Percentages*)

Total Assets Classes	1931	1932	1933
Under 50	42.7	60.1	36.0
50–100	52.2	68.5	33.5
100–250	60.9	68.4	38.6
250–500	67.9	71.2	38.7
500–1,000	73.6	73.9	43.5
1,000–5,000	78.5	79.2	52.9
5,000–10,000	86.1	87.4	60.6
10,000–50,000	88.9	92.4	77.8
50,000 and over	103.7	108.9	102.5
All corporations	90.4	95.7	76.0

a. Computed from data in *Statistics of Income:* 1931, pp. 156–157; 1932, pp. 162–163; 1933, pp. 168–169.

2. Cash dividends on common and preferred issues combined.

CHART 6

Ratio of Dividends to Net Income, by Assets Classes, 1933

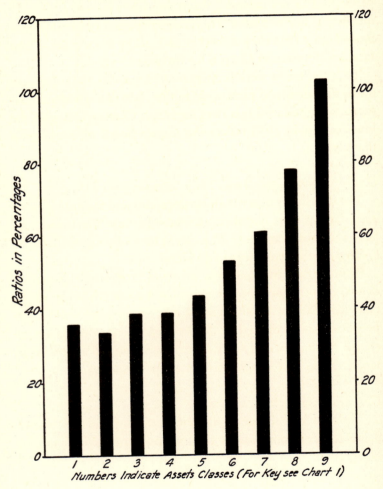

Ratios in Percentages

Numbers Indicate Assets Classes (For Key see Chart 1)

Dividends Rose with Increasing Assets Size

Table 20 shows that, with two unimportant breaks, the percentage of net income paid in dividends rose steadily with increasing size of assets. The giant corporations actually disbursed more than they earned in each of the three years. These facts are depicted in Chart 6 for the year 1933.

That the ratios were higher in 1932 than in 1931 does not mean that dividend rates were higher, but that dividend payments were reduced less than earnings. Correspondingly, the lower ratios in 1933 reflect the improvement of earnings in that year.

Unprofitable Corporations Show Similar Trend

The dividend ratios for all corporations and for unprofitable corporations have not been presented because they would appear as minus quantities.[3] This might be confusing as there can be no such thing as a minus dividend.

Unprofitable corporations, however, frequently pay dividends, drawing upon earned surpluses accumulated in previous years. When the dividend ratios for the unprofitable corporations are computed, it can be seen that as the classes increase in size their dividend payments become increasingly larger minus percentages of their annual deficits.

Variations Among Industries

Table 21 reveals the variations in the ratios of total dividends to net income among the four principal groups and the

3. Except for the giant class under all returns.

two manufacturing sub-groups for which data are available for each assets class separately.[4]

Five of the six groups covered by Table 21 display the same general dividend-ratio trend as do all industries combined. Except for total manufacturing, however, the individual series are more irregular. No clear cut relationship can be seen in finance.

The largest assets class shows the highest ratio—except in finance in each year and in metal and its products and in trade in 1931. In finance, the giant class shows the smallest ratio—a complete reversal of the all-industry picture.

The giants disbursed more in dividends than they earned, except in finance and trade in each year, and in total manufacturing and metal and its products in 1933. "Excess" dividends were also paid by the $5 million-to-$10 million class in metals in 1931 and 1932, and by the $10 million-to-$50 million class in the same industry in 1931.

The industries which, as a whole, distributed the largest percentages of their net income in dividends were chemicals and allied products in 1931 and 1932, and transportation and other public utilities in 1933. Finance made the smallest percentage distribution each year.

---

4. In Table 20, income and excess profits taxes have been deducted from net income. *Statistics of Income,* however, does not report the amount of these taxes by assets classes for the separate industries. Table 21, therefore, represents the net income available before payment of Federal income and excess profits taxes. For this reason the two tables are not strictly comparable. The relationship among the assets classes cannot, however, be appreciably affected by the inclusion or exclusion of income taxes, and the two tables may therefore be accepted as roughly comparable.

TABLE 21

RATIO OF TOTAL DIVIDENDS TO NET INCOME,[a] BY INDUSTRIAL GROUPS AND BY ASSETS CLASSES, 1931, 1932 AND 1933: PROFITABLE CORPORATIONS[b]

(Total Assets Classes in Thousands of Dollars; Ratios in Percentages)

Total Assets Classes	1931						1932						1933					
	A	B	C	D	E	F	A	B	C	D	E	F	A	B	C	D	E	F
Under 50	35.5	38.9	29.6	45.6	35.5	54.3	50.2	41.7	43.7	59.3	42.5	64.8	29.7	27.1	12.9	41.0	18.6	49.4
50–100	45.7	42.9	47.0	52.5	43.9	56.1	52.7	40.5	52.9	61.0	53.6	79.2	21.7	24.6	22.1	40.6	21.2	46.3
100–250	57.8	62.8	68.6	52.3	59.7	55.4	53.3	54.0	57.9	63.0	60.3	70.9	26.6	31.8	27.5	50.6	24.6	50.0
250–500	63.2	56.0	79.9	62.9	68.9	59.1	62.2	58.7	70.3	60.0	59.6	71.8	27.7	39.3	27.0	65.0	26.2	46.4
500–1,000	70.6	68.1	85.4	64.8	68.4	63.5	66.5	72.6	83.1	70.3	56.4	71.5	32.5	54.7	34.0	66.3	29.7	48.0
1,000–5,000	70.4	63.0	90.4	72.4	77.8	67.1	73.0	80.4	80.3	80.4	64.6	62.1	40.8	54.9	39.3	63.7	42.2	56.0
5,000–10,000	82.4	86.7	106.8	86.0	70.8	68.9	80.9	75.2	108.6	85.2	60.8	65.4	47.0	56.1	42.5	86.8	41.7	58.3
10,000–50,000	88.3	76.3	101.5	92.3	53.6	64.9	87.9	95.1	99.7	96.6	53.1	60.1	66.3	97.7	72.6	93.2	48.2	58.3
50,000 and over	101.6	134.1	101.3	107.0	70.9	46.2	114.0	141.3	110.3	106.7	87.1	33.1	92.5	127.3	76.7	109.0	49.7	45.3
All corporations	87.9	105.1	98.0	101.8	64.6	58.2	93.1	112.4	96.2	101.8	67.1	52.8	62.5	94.2	63.1	101.5	38.5	52.2

LEGEND: A = Total manufacturing. B = Chemicals and allied products. C = Metal and its products. D = Transportation and other public utilities. E = Trade. F = Finance.

a. See footnote 4, p. 80.
b. Computed from data in *Statistics of Income:* 1931, pp. 161, 169–170, 173, 175; 1932, pp. 167, 175–176, 179, 181; 1933, pp. 173, 181, 183, 185–186, 188.

Explanation of Dividend-Ratio Trend

The most plausible explanation of the general trend that has been discussed, is that with increasing size there comes increasing ability to pay dividends in bad years. This is evidenced by the fact that, as Table 22 proves, surplus and undivided profits accumulated in previous years of prosperity are a larger percentage of the total capitalization of large corporations than of small ones.

TABLE 22

RATIO OF NET SURPLUS AND UNDIVIDED PROFITS TO TOTAL
CAPITALIZATION, BY ASSETS CLASSES, 1931,
1932 AND 1933[a,b]

(Total Assets Classes in Thousands of Dollars; Ratios in Percentages)

Total Assets Classes	All Returns			Returns Showing Net Income			Returns Showing No Net Income		
	1931	1932	1933	1931	1932	1933	1931	1932	1933
Under 50	−32.9	−51.7	−51.9	12.5	3.7	4.9	−71.1	−67.5	−78.1
50–100	1.4	− 5.3	− 4.9	21.6	19.6	20.4	−14.2	−12.5	−17.0
100–250	8.5	3.8	3.5	24.0	23.7	24.7	− 3.0	− 2.1	− 6.8
250–500	14.7	11.6	11.5	28.1	30.4	30.0	5.4	5.5	1.9
500–1,000	17.8	15.0	15.4	30.6	31.6	32.3	9.8	9.4	6.2
1,000–5,000	23.1	20.7	20.6	34.0	33.0	33.0	16.8	16.5	13.8
5,000–10,000	26.4	23.0	22.9	35.9	35.1	35.4	20.8	18.0	15.4
10,000–50,000	25.3	22.7	24.2	31.1	26.9	30.1	21.0	20.8	20.0
50,000 and over	26.2	23.2	23.3	28.4	23.4	22.4	24.7	30.1	23.9
All corporations	23.2	19.9	20.2	29.5	26.0	26.2	18.9	17.4	16.5

a. Computed from data in *Statistics of Income*, page references same as for Table 2.
b. Net surplus and undivided profits equal surplus and undivided profits less the deficits of corporations which report deficits instead of surpluses. Minus signs indicate net deficits for the class.

Ratio of Surplus and Undivided Profits to Total Capitalization

Table 22 demonstrates that the larger corporations have a greater percentage of their total capitalization in the form of net surplus and undivided profits than the smaller. For the unprofitable corporations the trend is steadily upward through the largest assets class. The smallest three classes show net deficits in each of the three years. For the profitable corporations the trend is upward through the $5 million-to-$10 million class, and then reverses its direction through the highest two classes. When all returns are considered, the $5 million-to-$10 million class made the best record in 1931; the $50 million-and-over class, in 1932; and $10 million-to-$50 million, in 1933. The giants were close seconds in both 1931 and 1933.

C. RATIO OF DIVIDENDS TO NET WORTH AND TO COMMON STOCK

Table 23 shows the ratio of total dividends to net worth—the stockholders' equity—and the ratio of common dividends to that portion of the equity which is represented by common stock. For 1933, the facts are brought out in Chart 7.

Table 23 reveals a tendency for the ratios of total dividends to net worth to increase as the assets classes increase. This is true of all three years and of all three groups. The tendency, however, commences only with the second, third or fourth smallest class. The under-$50,000 class is out of order. Among unprofitable corporations in 1933 it shows the largest ratio. For the other eight series of figures it shows a larger ratio

CHART 7

RATIO OF TOTAL DIVIDENDS TO NET WORTH AND RATIO OF ESTIMATED COMMON DIVIDENDS TO COMMON STOCK, BY ASSETS CLASSES, 1933

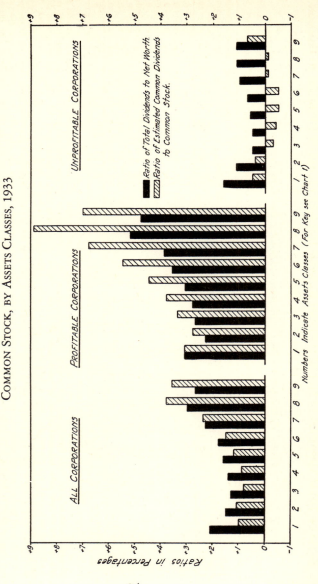

TABLE 23

Ratio of Total Dividends to Net Worth and Ratio of Estimated Common Dividends to Common Stock, by Assets Classes, 1931, 1932 and 1933[a]

(Total Assets Classes in Thousands of Dollars; Ratios in Percentages)

Total Assets Classes	Ratio of Total Dividends to Net Worth									Ratio of Common Dividends to Common Stock[b]								
	All Returns			Returns Showing Net Income			Returns Showing No Net Income			All Returns			Returns Showing Net Income			Returns Showing No Net Income		
	1931	1932	1933	1931	1932	1933	1931	1932	1933	1931	1932	1933	1931	1932	1933	1931	1932	1933
Under 50	3.4	2.1	2.1	4.9	5.2	3.1	2.0	1.1	1.6	2.3	1.0	1.0	5.7	5.4	3.1	0.7	0.3	0.5
50–100	2.5	1.7	1.5	4.1	4.3	2.3	1.2	0.8	1.1	2.3	1.2	1.1	5.5	5.5	2.8	0.6	0.3	0.4
100–250	2.6	1.7	1.3	4.3	4.1	2.7	1.3	0.8	0.5	2.6	1.2	0.8	6.0	5.6	3.4	0.7	0.1	-0.3c
250–500	2.8	1.8	1.4	4.6	4.3	2.8	1.3	0.9	0.5	3.0	1.5	0.9	7.2	6.7	3.8	0.7	0.1	-0.4c
500–1,000	2.8	1.9	1.6	4.8	4.4	3.1	1.4	1.0	0.6	3.1	1.6	1.2	7.9	7.0	4.5	0.7	0.1	-0.5c
1,000–5,000	3.0	2.1	1.8	5.1	4.4	3.6	1.7	1.2	0.7	3.7	2.0	1.5	9.0	7.4	5.5	1.2	0.3	-0.5c
5,000–10,000	3.7	2.6	2.3	6.1	5.1	3.9	2.2	1.4	1.0	5.5	3.0	2.4	11.6	9.5	6.8	2.2	0.6	-0.1c
10,000–50,000	4.0	2.9	3.0	6.2	5.4	5.2	2.3	1.7	1.1	5.9	3.5	3.8	11.1	8.9	8.9	2.1	1.0	-0.1c
50,000 and over	5.2	3.5	2.7	7.3	5.8	4.8	3.7	2.2	1.1	9.0	5.0	3.6	13.4	9.1	7.0	5.8	2.7	0.7
All corporations	4.3	2.9	2.4	6.3	5.4	4.4	2.7	1.7	1.0	6.2	3.5	2.7	11.1	8.5	6.5	3.1	1.3	0.2

a. Computed from data in *Statistics of Income*, page references same as for Table 2.

b. Ratios of dividends to common stock were computed on the assumption that the dividends paid on the preferred stock averaged 6 per cent for all assets classes in each of the three groups and in each of the three years. Some assumption of this sort was necessary in order to estimate the rate of return on common stock, because *Statistics of Income* does not report preferred and common stock dividends separately. The ratio of common dividends to common stock was computed after first deducting from total cash dividends paid an amount equal to 6 per cent on the preferred stock. To bring out the relationship between classes, the particular rate selected to represent the preferred stock dividends is of no great importance. The table, however, unquestionably distorts this relationship to some unknown extent, owing to the fact that there must have been some variations in the preferred dividend rate among the different assets classes; between the three years; and between profitable and unprofitable corporations, year for year and class for class. It should also be noted that the common stockholders' right to surplus and undivided profits has not been considered; and, furthermore, that the amount of preferred stock in relation to the amount of common varies from class to class.

The reader is, therefore, urged to interpret the right-hand division of Table 23 with great caution. The figures should not be used to draw conclusions as to the rate of common stock dividends actually paid. They should not be made the basis of conclusions as to differences between years or between profitable and unprofitable corporations. Their only value is to show the relationship among assets classes, separately for each of the three groups of returns, and separately for each of the three years. Even in this respect the ratios represent only reasonable estimates.

c. Minus ratios indicate that the assumed 6 per cent payments on preferred stock accounted for more than the total cash dividends shown in *Statistics of Income*.

than the four to six next higher classes. In 1931 and 1932 the $50 million-and-over class stands at the head of the list; in 1933 this class is near the top. On the whole, the larger corporations paid larger dividends in relation to their net worth than the smaller ones. The ratios of common dividends to common stock[5] present a more clearly marked trend of increasing ratios with increasing assets size, but these ratios must be regarded with great caution.

Variations Among Industries

Table 24 is presented to give some idea of the variations among industrial groups in the ratio of dividends to net worth in the year 1933.

In general there is a tendency, in all industries except finance, for the dividend ratio to increase with increasing assets size. In every case, however, the trend is highly irregular. Nowhere is it sharply defined—especially not in the unprofitable group.

In finance the highest ratio appears in either the smallest or the second smallest class. Another important deviation from the general pattern is found among the unprofitable trade corporations which show by far the highest ratio in the smallest class. The sharp reversal of the trend that occurs in the chemical industry in the highest class under profitable corporations and under all corporations, is also noteworthy. Under unprofitable corporations, however, the largest chemical concerns show the highest dividend ratios.

The giant class is in the lead in only 5 out of 18 possible

5. See footnote b to Table 23.

TABLE 24

RATIO OF TOTAL DIVIDENDS TO NET WORTH, BY INDUSTRIAL GROUPS AND BY ASSETS CLASSES, 1933[a]

(Total Assets Classes in Thousands of Dollars; Ratios in Percentages)

Total Assets Classes	All Returns						Returns Showing Net Income						Returns Showing No Net Income					
	A	B	C	D	E	F	A	B	C	D	E	F	A	B	C	D	E	F
Under 50	1.4	1.7	0.7	3.2	2.1	2.7	3.0	3.7	1.1	4.9	1.6	4.9	0.6	0.5	0.6	1.1	2.5	1.6
50–100	1.0	1.5	0.7	2.6	0.9	2.9	2.0	2.9	1.8	4.5	1.5	3.1	0.4	0.1	0.2	0.5	0.4	2.9
100–250	1.4	2.2	0.9	2.7	1.1	1.3	2.5	3.6	2.2	4.2	1.7	3.2	0.4	0.7	0.2	0.6	0.5	0.6
250–500	1.6	3.0	1.0	3.6	1.2	1.0	2.7	4.6	2.2	5.4	2.0	2.5	0.5	0.7	0.4	0.5	0.3	0.5
500–1,000	1.9	4.9	1.2	3.3	1.5	1.1	3.2	7.0	2.5	4.9	2.4	2.5	0.5	1.0	0.4	0.8	0.4	0.6
1,000–5,000	2.2	4.5	1.2	3.1	2.3	1.4	3.6	5.9	2.5	4.4	3.5	3.0	0.6	0.6	0.5	0.5	0.6	0.9
5,000–10,000	2.7	6.7	2.0	3.2	2.3	1.8	4.5	8.8	3.2	5.1	3.3	2.8	0.9	1.4	1.3	0.3	1.0	1.4
10,000–50,000	3.3	8.0	1.8	3.9	2.6	2.5	5.7	11.0	4.5	5.7	4.2	4.0	0.6	0.2	0.7	0.7	0.4	2.0
50,000 and over	2.9	2.8	1.9	2.8	4.0	2.4	4.5	3.3	5.1	5.2	5.0	3.7	0.9	1.7	0.4	0.8	1.0	2.2
All corporations	2.7	3.7	1.7	2.9	2.2	2.0	4.4	4.7	4.2	5.2	3.3	3.3	0.7	1.5	0.5	0.8	0.8	1.6

LEGEND: A = Total manufacturing. B = Chemicals and allied products. C = Metal and its products. D = Transportation and other public utilities. E = Trade. F = Finance.

a. Computed from data in Statistics of Income for 1933, page references same as for Table 7.

instances; the sub-giants, in 7. In 14 instances the lowest ratios appear in the smallest or second smallest class.

For all classes combined, chemicals have the highest ratio under all returns, transportation and other public utilities under profitable corporations, and finance—by a very narrow margin—under unprofitable returns. Metal has the lowest ratio under all returns and under unprofitable corporations; trade and finance, under profitable corporations.

Each industry, on the whole, shows a higher ratio for its profitable than for its unprofitable corporations. The difference is widest for transportation and other public utilities and narrowest for finance.

Chapter 9

SPECIAL CONSIDERATION OF BANKING
PROFITS

IN THE preceding volume of this series,[1] a special chapter was devoted to banking[2] because of the important influence exercised by the banking mechanism upon industry and business. For the same reason, there is included in the present volume a brief analysis of the profitableness of commercial banking operations.[3]

Profitableness of National Banks as a Whole

Comprehensive figures on the trend of profitableness are available only for national banks. They show that for these banks as a whole the rate of net profits on capital funds[4] was without any definite tendency—up or down—between 1900

1. *Big Business: Its Growth and Its Place.*
2. *Ibid.,* Chap. 6.
3. This analysis is not based on data from *Statistics of Income,* but on other material, as indicated.
4. Net profits (net additions to profits before dividends) represent gross earnings from operations, less current expenses and net losses. If these deductions exceed gross earnings, the result is a (net) deficit.
Capital funds consist of book value of common capital stock, surplus and undivided profits; reserves for contingencies; and reserves for stock dividends payable on common stock. For the years 1933–1936, capital funds include also preferred stock (A and B) and retirement fund for preferred stock.

and 1911 (between 7.5 per cent and 9.5 per cent), definitely downward from 1911 until 1916 (from 7.5 per cent in 1912 to 6 per cent in 1915), but constantly upward from 1916 (7.5 per cent) to 1920 (10.8 per cent). During the next decade profits were on a lower level, ranging from 6.5 per cent in 1923 to 8.2 per cent in 1929. They dropped to 6.2 per cent in 1930 and 1.4 per cent in 1931. In 1932, 1933 and 1934 there were deficits which amounted to 4.3, 7.8 and 10.1 per cent, respectively. Net profits of 2.3 per cent were earned in 1935, and of 7.6 per cent in 1936.[5]

The average rate of net profits was 8.3 per cent between September 1, 1900 and June 30, 1911; 7.2 per cent during the next four-year period; 9.4 per cent between July 1, 1915 and June 30, 1920; and 7.3 per cent between July 1, 1920 and June 30, 1930.

In order to obtain a more comprehensive picture of the profitableness of commercial banking operations, the Federal Reserve Committee[6] made a study of the earning reports of national banks for the five-year period ending June 30, 1930. The average number of reporting banks was 7,403. Of this number, 4,000 banks, with loans and investments of more than 50 per cent of the total loans and investments of these

---

5. Cf. Report of the Federal Reserve Committee on Branch, Group and Chain Banking, on *Banking Profits, 1890–1931*.

The percentages given in the Committee's report for 1890–1931, as well as those for 1932–1936, are based on figures in the annual reports of the United States Comptroller of the Currency. For the period 1900–1906, data are for fiscal years ending August 31; for 1907, for the ten months from September 1, 1906 to June 30, 1907; for 1908 to 1936, for fiscal years ending June 30. Capital funds are as of the end of the fiscal year.

6. See footnote 5.

7,403 banks, made net profits of 6 per cent or more, 1,396 banks made from 3 up to 6 per cent, 836 made up to 3 per cent, while 1,171 had deficits.

Profitableness of National Banks Grouped by Size of Loans and Investments

Table 25 presents the numerical and percentage distribution of the 7,403 national banks, grouped by size of loans and investments and by several profit classifications. Chart 8 shows the percentage distribution.

It appears that the largest percentage of banks recording deficits—35 per cent—occurred among the group of smallest banks. As the banks increased in size, the proportion of unprofitable institutions decreased continuously.

In the group of banks earning profits up to 3 per cent, the range was from 19 per cent of the total number in the smallest loans-and-investments-class to 5 per cent of the number in the largest class; while in the group earning profits from 3–5.9 per cent, the range was from 20 to 13 per cent. Only 26 per cent of the banks in the smallest group made profits of 6 per cent or more, but 80 per cent of the largest banks attained that level of earnings.

A better way to show the poor record of the smaller institutions is to point out that while in the smallest class 35 per cent of the banks made no profits, the corresponding figures for the banks with loans and investments of $150,000 to $500,000 were 22 per cent, for the $500,000-to-$1,000,000 banks 14 per cent, for the $1 million-to-$5 million banks 10 per cent, and for the $5 million-and-over class 6 per cent.

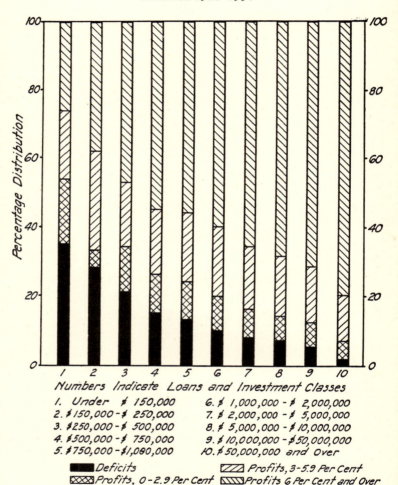

CHART 8

PERCENTAGE DISTRIBUTION OF NET PROFITS OF 7,403 NATIONAL
BANKS, BY LOANS-AND-INVESTMENT CLASSES,
AVERAGE 1926–1930

Percentage Distribution

Numbers Indicate Loans and Investment Classes

1. Under $ 150,000	6. $ 1,000,000 - $ 2,000,000
2. $150,000 - $ 250,000	7. $ 2,000,000 - $ 5,000,000
3. $250,000 - $ 500,000	8. $ 5,000,000 - $ 10,000,000
4. $500,000 - $ 750,000	9. $ 10,000,000 - $50,000,000
5. $750,000 - $1,000,000	10. $ 50,000,000 and Over

Deficits   Profits, 3-5.9 Per Cent

Profits, 0 - 2.9 Per Cent   Profits 6 Per Cent and Over

92

TABLE 25

NUMBER AND PERCENTAGE DISTRIBUTION OF 7,403 NATIONAL BANKS, BY SIZE OF LOANS AND INVESTMENTS AND BY RATE OF NET PROFITS ON INVESTED CAPITAL, AVERAGE 1926–1930[a]

(Loans-and-Investments Classes in Thousands of Dollars)

Loans-and-Investments Classes	Distribution by Number						Percentage in Each Class					
	Deficits	Profits 0–2.9 Per Cent	Profits 3–5.9 Per Cent	Deficits, or Profits its Under 6 Per Cent[b]	Profits 6 Per Cent and Over	Total[c]	Deficits	Profits 0–2.9 Per Cent	Profits 3–5.9 Per Cent	Deficits, or Prof-its Under 6 Per Cent[b]	Profits 6 Per Cent and Over	Total[c]
Under 150	123	66	72	261	92	353	35	19	20	74	26	100
150–250	207	114	139	460	281	741	28	15	19	62	38	100
250–500	333	206	314	853	766	1,619	21	13	19	53	47	100
500–750	153	120	198	471	582	1,053	15	11	19	45	55	100
750–1,000	96	81	141	318	407	725	13	11	20	44	56	100
1,000–2,000	140	133	260	533	797	1,330	10	10	20	40	60	100
2,000–5,000	86	77	181	344	675	1,019	8	8	18	34	66	100
5,000–10,000	21	23	53	97	215	312	7	7	17	31	69	100
10,000–50,000	11	14	33	58	153	211	5	7	16	28	72	100
50,000 and over	1	2	5	8	32	40	2	5	13	20	80	100
All banks	1,171	836	1,396	3,403	4,000	7,403	16	11	19	46	54	100

a. Reconstructed from data in Report of the Federal Reserve Committee on Branch, Group and Chain Banking, op. cit.
b. Sum of three preceding columns.
c. Sum of two preceding columns.

For the 0–2.9 per cent profit group the corresponding percentages were 19, 14, 11, 9 and 7, respectively; for the 3–5.9 per cent profit group: 20, 19, 19, 19, 16; and for the class of banks earning 6 per cent or more: 26, 44, 56, 63 and 71.

If these percentages are compared with the averages for each profit group, it will be noted that among banks with less than $500,000 loans and investments (the first three classes in Table 25), the proportion with profits was smaller than the average. Conversely, among each of these three classes of smallest banks the proportion with deficits was larger than the average.

Net profits of less than 6 per cent are probably not sufficient to enable a bank to pay dividends and set aside adequate reserves. Therefore, 74 per cent of the smallest banks may be said to have had inadequate profits. For the next two larger groups the percentages were 62 and 53, respectively. Of the 7,403 banks as a whole, only 46 per cent made profits of less than 6 per cent, indicating again the poor showing of banks with less than $500,000 loans and investments. It should be noted, however, that banks with loans and investments of $500,000 to $1,000,000 barely measure up to the average. Over two-thirds of the banks that made profits of less than 6 per cent had less than $1 million loans and investments. These banks constituted 53 per cent of the total number of banks of that size.

Net Profits of National Banks by Geographical Regions

A comparison of the profitableness of national banks of different sizes classified by certain geographical regions shows a favorable record for the larger banks similar to that for the group of 7,403 banks as a whole. This is demonstrated by Table 26, which gives for five regions the percentage of banks in each size class which had deficits, or net profits of less than

TABLE 26

PERCENTAGE DISTRIBUTION OF NATIONAL BANKS REPORTING NET DEFICITS, OR NET PROFITS OF LESS THAN 3 PER CENT, BY SIZE OF LOANS AND INVESTMENTS AND BY GEOGRAPHICAL REGIONS, AVERAGE 1926–1930[a]

(*Loans-and-Investments Classes in Thousands of Dollars*)

Loans-and-Investments Classes	Percentages				
	Northeastern States[b]	Mid-Continent States[c]	North Central States[d]	Southeastern States[e]	Western States[f]
Under 150	51.7	51.4	53.2	57.7	63.3
150–250	32.5	47.8	31.5	36.4	49.4
250–500	24.2	38.4	32.9	26.4	34.6
500–750	19.1	32.9	25.8	23.3	26.9
750–1,000	18.7	31.5	24.4	25.3	24.9
1,000–2,000	15.2	30.6	22.0	20.7	25.0
2,000–5,000	12.8	18.2	17.0	20.7	23.8
5,000 and over	12.2	11.2	9.6	17.0	18.9
All banks	16.9	37.0	25.2	24.7	32.5

a. Source same as for Table 25.

b. Maine, New Hampshire, Vermont, Massachusetts, Rhode Island, Connecticut, New York, New Jersey, Delaware, Pennsylvania, Maryland, District of Columbia.

c. Minnesota, North Dakota, South Dakota, Iowa, Nebraska, Missouri, Kansas, Louisiana, Texas, Arkansas, Oklahoma.

d. Michigan, Wisconsin, Illinois, Indiana, Ohio.

e. West Virginia, Virginia, Kentucky, Tennessee, North Carolina, South Carolina, Georgia, Florida, Alabama, Mississippi.

f. Montana, Idaho, Wyoming, Colorado, New Mexico, Arizona, Utah, Nevada, Washington, Oregon, California.

3 per cent. It should be noted that, as a whole, banks in the smallest three classes made their best showing in the northeastern states and their worst in the western states.

Profitableness of State Banks as Indicated by Results in Iowa

No comprehensive figures are available on the comparative profitableness of state commercial banks of various size. However, the Federal Reserve Committee's report, referred to above, contains a study of about a thousand Iowa state banks for the same period as that covered by the analysis of the 7,403 national banks. This study indicates that among state banks the smaller institutions also had the poorer earnings record. Indeed, the profitableness of Iowa state banks was not only less favorable than that of the 7,403 national banks as a whole, but also than that of national banks in the mid-continent states, of which Iowa forms a part.

It can be seen from Table 27 that 42 per cent of the smallest Iowa state banks had deficits, as against only 35 per cent of the smallest national banks and 36 per cent of the smallest mid-continent national banks. In every class for which comparisons can be made, Iowa banks show up worse than the 7,403 national banks as a whole; and, but for a few minor exceptions, worse than the mid-continent national banks. For the three groups as a whole, the percentage of unprofitable banks is 31 for state institutions in Iowa, 24 for national banks in the 11 mid-continent states, and 16 for the 7,403 national banks. The same general relationship among the three groups exists for those banks which earned net profits of less than 3 per cent.

When the picture is viewed from the opposite angle, it appears that the percentage of the most profitable banks in each class was lower for Iowa state banks than for either of the two other groups. In the smallest loans-and-investments class only 21 per cent of the Iowa banks made net profits of 6 per cent or more, while this level of profitableness was reached by 29 per cent of the smallest mid-continent national

TABLE 27

PERCENTAGE DISTRIBUTION OF NATIONAL BANKS, MID-CONTINENT NATIONAL BANKS AND IOWA STATE BANKS, BY SIZE OF LOANS AND INVESTMENTS AND BY RATE OF NET PROFITS ON INVESTED CAPITAL, AVERAGE 1926–1930[a]

(*Loans-and-Investments Classes in Thousands of Dollars*)

Loans-and-Investments Classes	Percentages											
	Deficits			Profits								
				0–2.9 Per Cent			3–5.9 Per Cent			6 Per Cent and Over		
	A	B	C	A	B	C	A	B	C	A	B	C
Under 150	35	36	42	19	16	20	20	19	17	26	29	21
150–250	28	32	34	15	16	19	19	14	17	38	38	30
250–500	21	25	29	13	13	16	19	16	18	47	46	37
500–750	15	20	20	11	13	16	19	16	20	55	51	44
750–1,000	13	18	18	11	13	17	20	16	18	56	53	47
1,000–2,000	10	17	19	10	14	18	20	17	19	60	52	45
2,000 and over[b]	8	10	13	8	9	10	17	20	25	66	71	52
5,000 and over	6	4	–	7	7	–	16	17	–	71	72	–
All banks	16	24	31	11	13	18	19	16	18	54	47	33

LEGEND: A = 7,403 national banks. B = Mid-continent national banks. C = Iowa state banks.

a. Reconstructed from source cited in Table 25.
b. For national banks, $2,000,000 to $5,000,000.

banks and by 26 per cent of the smallest of the 7,403 national banks. For all size classes combined, the corresponding figures are 33, 47 and 54 per cent, respectively.

Gross Earnings of Large and Small Banks[7]

Up to this point the discussion of profitableness of banks has been in terms of net profits on invested capital. It was shown that the larger banks have had a much better record than the smaller ones.

Turning now to a comparison of gross earnings and of expenses as between banks of different sizes it appears that the smallest banks have generally had higher rates of gross earnings in relation to their total earning assets or loans and investments than the larger ones. There was, however, by no means a constant decrease in these rates as banks advanced in size;[8,9] but in those cases where banks of different sizes showed more or less the same rates of gross earnings, there

7. The following review is based on the earnings reports of 7,403 national banks for the years 1926–1930, of member banks in the Chicago Federal Reserve district for 1926 and 1928, in the Richmond district for 1926, in the San Francisco district for 1928, in the Philadelphia district for 1929 and 1934, in the Cleveland district for 1926–1935, and in the Dallas district for 1929, 1933, 1934 and 1935.

8. Indeed, in the case of state banks and trust companies in the Philadelphia district during 1929, for instance, rates of gross earnings increased as banks advanced in size, while among national banks there was no definite tendency. Earnings reports for 1934 for national banks showed a decline in rates of gross earnings as banks advanced in size, but among state banks and trust companies the reverse was the case, although the tendency was very irregular.

9. It should further be noted that among banks with more or less identical ratios between time and gross deposits, rates of gross earnings tend to be on closely the same level, irrespective of size of the bank. For a detailed analysis see *Circular No. 470,* May 12, 1930, issued by the Federal Reserve Bank of Philadelphia.

was a distinct tendency for the larger banks to show the greater rates of net profits.

High Gross Earnings Versus Low Net Profits

There is no single, definite explanation to account for the fact that high gross earnings often result in low net profits, while low gross earnings may produce high net profits. Nevertheless, several general conclusions can be drawn from an analysis of the available data.

In terms of earning assets or loans and investments, total operating expenses were generally higher among the smaller than among the larger banks. Significant exceptions occurred, namely, in those cases where the advantage, gained by the larger banks because of relatively lower expenses for salaries and wages, was offset by higher expenses for interest paid on deposits.[10] On the whole, however, for each of the several groups of banks analyzed the net earnings[11] rate was not highest among the largest banks, but it was generally higher than the average for each group.

Other income, such as profits on securities sold and recoveries on bonds, stocks, other securities and miscellaneous charged-off assets, did not show a general and definite tendency to increase as banks advanced in size. Many differences occurred among the several groups of banks. Losses[12] how-

10. Again it should be noted that among banks with identical ratios of time deposits to gross deposits, interest expense tends to be equal, irrespective of the size of the banks.

11. Gross earnings less current expenses of operations.

12. Includes losses on loans; stocks; miscellaneous losses; and depreciation on banking-house furniture and fixtures.

ever, were distinctly larger among the smaller banks. Therefore, in those cases where income exceeded losses, the net
earnings of the larger banks were increased by a larger amount
than was the case among the smaller banks; and, where losses
exceeded other income, the net result was to decrease the net
earnings of the former by a smaller amount than was the case
among the latter. Thus, notwithstanding higher rates of gross
earnings, the smaller banks had definitely lower rates of net
profits—in terms of loans and investments—than the larger
banks.

Earning Assets in Relationship to Invested Capital

The greater profitableness[13] of the larger banks should
further be considered in connection with the fact that earning
assets per hundred dollars of invested capital showed a distinct tendency to increase as the banks advanced in size. As
a consequence, net profits on invested capital generally increased from a minimum for the smaller banks to a maximum
for the banks with the larger loans and investments.

Operating Results in Relation to Ratio of Time Deposits to Total Deposits

A few further remarks, qualifying to some extent the above
conclusions, should be made regarding the operating results
of banks having different ratios of time deposits to total
deposits. From a review of the earning reports of national
banks in the Philadelphia district for the year 1929, it appears

13. I.e., net profits in terms of earning assets or loans and investments.

that gross earnings showed fairly little fluctuation not only among banks of different size,[14] but also among banks of the same size but with different ratios of time deposits to gross deposits. The net results of operations were definitely in favor of the larger banks. Within each group of banks in the several time-to-gross-deposits classifications, the range of net profits among banks of different size was, however, considerably narrower than it was among all banks not so classified.

14. However, 1934 earnings reports showed a tendency for gross earnings ratios to be larger among smaller banks.

PART THREE

PROFITS OF GROUPS OF LARGE
CORPORATIONS

Chapter 10

PROFITS OF GROUPS OF LARGE NON-FINANCIAL CORPORATIONS, 1900–1934

A. 1900–1914

Were the Early Trusts Profitable?

To ascertain whether the large industrial corporations formed during the "trust" movement preceding 1904 were profitable to investors, a study was made of 93, each of which had a total capitalization[1] of $10 million or more in 1903.[2] For only 34 of these corporations, however, was information available on stated capital and earnings, as well as on divi-

---

1. The 93 companies were from a list of all non-financial corporations, mentioned either by John Moody in *The Truth About the Trusts* or by the National Industrial Conference Board in *Mergers in Industry,* that at some time between 1900 and 1903 had $10 million or over of capital, as represented by the par value of their stocks and bonds. Of this list, fairly complete information was obtainable for only 34; for 59 others information was available concerning dividends and stock prices only. In addition there were 16 other corporations for which definite statements were available that they had failed between 1901 and 1914 with loss to their common stockholders. It should be noted that capitalization, and not assets, is used as a measure of size. There is undoubtedly, however, a high degree of correlation between the two.

2. Bonds have been included in capitalization because, although they represent borrowed funds, they involve a participation in the risks, unlike bank loans which are only temporary advances and usually secured without regard to the actual profits of the borrower. Furthermore, in many cases bonds represent the greater part of the money investment. If bonds are included in capitalization, the interest paid on them must be regarded as earnings.

dends and stock prices.[3]

For these 34 corporations, the average ratio of net earnings[4] to stated capital,[5] over a period varying from 7 to 14 years for the separate companies, ranged from 1.6 per cent (Allis-Chalmers Manufacturing Company) to 12.3 per cent (General Electric Company). Average earnings of 6 per cent or more were reached by only 9 of the 34 companies. The best results for the 34 companies as a whole were in 1902, 1906 and 1907, in each of which years about 7.25 per cent was earned on total capitalization;[6] the poorest results came in 1904, when earnings dropped to 4.2 per cent.

On their common stock issues, 9 of the 34 corporations paid no dividends for periods ranging up to 14 years. Only 6 averaged 5 per cent or more. At the top of the list was the American Tobacco Company, with average common stock dividends of 17.9 per cent of par value. The average dividend paid by the 34 companies was 2.7 per cent on the par value of their common stock. If a supplementary list of 59 large

3. The abbreviated names of the 34 companies are: Allis-Chalmers; Amalgamated Copper; American Agricultural Chemical; American Can; American Car and Foundry; American Locomotive; American Smelting and Refining; American Sugar Refining; American Tobacco; American Woolen; American Writing Paper; Cambria Steel; Colorado Fuel and Iron; Corn Products Refining; Crucible Steel; du Pont; General Electric; Harbison-Walker Refractories; International Harvester; International Mercantile Marine; International Paper; Lackawanna Steel; National Biscuit; National Enameling and Stamping; Pressed Steel Car; Pullman; Quaker Oats; Republic Iron and Steel; Sloss-Sheffield Steel and Iron Standard Milling; Union Bag and Paper; United States Rubber; United States Steel; Virginia-Carolina Chemical.

4. Net earnings available for dividends plus interest charges on bonded indebtedness. Some adjustments have been made where "hidden" depreciation, obsolescence, profits or losses were discovered.

5. Bonds, stocks and surplus.

6. 7.26 per cent in 1902; 7.24 per cent in 1906 and 7.25 per cent in 1907.

industrial corporations[7] is added to the 34, it appears that the 93 corporations, as a whole, paid common stock dividends between 1900 and 1914 averaging 4.3 per cent, with 24 paying nothing. Only 16 companies paid as much as 7 per cent, and only 22 paid as high a rate on their par value as could have been obtained from industrial bonds at the time—5 per cent.

The usual rate promised on the preferred stock of the 73 companies that had preferred stock outstanding, was 7 per cent. Only 39 of the companies, however, paid at the promised rate, including some that postponed their payments or paid in scrip. The average rate actually paid was 5.3 per cent. The International Mercantile Marine Company paid nothing on its 6 per cent preferred during the 12 years covered. Over a period of 15 years, the American Writing Paper Company paid an annual average of only 0.8 per cent on its 7 per cent issue.

Between 1900[8] and 1914[9] the market value[10] of the 34 common stocks[11] advanced in 19 cases and declined in 15. For the 93 companies, there were 48 declines and 45 advances. But the gains to stockholders in the successful companies were so great that an investment evenly spread over the whole 93 would have been very profitable. Instances of large advances in the prices of common stocks are: Ameri-

7. Companies for which data on earnings or capitalization were lacking.
8. 1901 in 5 cases; 1902 in 2 cases; 1903 in 2 cases; and 1905, 1906 and 1908 in one case each.
9. 1912 in one case and 1913 in another.
10. Average of high and low prices for each year.
11. Allowing for exchanges, split-ups, stock dividends, changes in par value, etc.

can Car and Foundry Company, from $16.49 to $48.93 (196.7 per cent) ; American Tobacco Company, from $99.16 to $233.99 (136 per cent) ; General Electric Company, from $138.40 to $314.51 (127.2 per cent) ; Harbison-Walker Refractories Company, from $4.83 (1903) to $49.63 (927.5 per cent) ; National Biscuit Company, from $33.89 to $128.63 (279.6 per cent) ; Quaker Oats Company, from $41.62 to $240.00 (476.6 per cent) ; and Standard Milling Company, from $5.50 (1901) to $38.50 (600 per cent).

How the Investor Fared

An investor who in 1900[12] bought 100 shares of each of the 93 companies, at the average price of the year, would have paid about $499,000.[13] In 1914[14] his investment would have been worth approximately $704,000, at that year's average prices. He would have received about $470,000 in dividends, or at an annual rate of about 6.7 per cent on the original investment. Counting appreciation, the investor's annual return, though very irregular, would have reached the decidedly satisfactory average of about 9 per cent.[15] But allowance should be made for 16 more companies with capitalization of $10 million or more which failed before 1914 with loss to their stockholders, and in most cases to their creditors, but which had to be omitted from the study

12. Or in the first subsequent year in which the stock was publicly quoted.
13. Disregarding commissions.
14. Or the last preceding year in which the stock had any market.
15. Appreciation was computed by the compound interest formula, because it is not realized until the stock is sold.

because their securities were not quoted on any stock exchange. It is extremely likely that the average yield on an investment in 100 shares of each of the 109 corporations would have been less than 8 per cent, counting dividends, appreciation and losses together; and this yield would have been derived from 45 companies as the others were unprofitable.

If the investor had invested an equal amount of money in each of the companies, instead of buying an equal number of shares, his yield in dividends and appreciation would have been much less, because a smaller proportion of his total investment would have been in the higher priced stocks of 1900 which, as a whole, did better over the period than the lower priced ones.

Results of Other Studies

Similar studies have been made by A. S. Dewing[16] and by the National Industrial Conference Board, Inc.,[17] but they were confined to mergers.

Dewing's conclusions, based on an analysis of 35 consolidations for ten-year periods, were that in most cases the earnings of the mergers in their first ten years of existence failed to come up to their promoters' promises: " . . . after sufficient time had elapsed to permit the consolidation to perfect its organization, to reconstruct its plant and to effect all the anticipated economies of combination and large-scale produc-

16. "A Statistical Test of the Success of Consolidations," Quarterly Journal of Economics, November 1921, pp. 84–101.
17. Mergers in Industry.

tion, and after considerable sums of new money had been invested in betterments and in new plants, the earnings gradually diminished until they were no more, perhaps a little less, than during the first year of consolidation. And the first-year earnings, as has been shown already, were less than the earnings of the separate plants before consolidation."[18]

The National Industrial Conference Board's study of consolidations, numbering from 29 to 48 in the various years from 1900 through 1913,[19] concludes that "In none of the years did any of the enterprises make extraordinary returns and comparatively few made as much as 10%. On the other hand, there was in all years a considerable number whose returns were less than 2½% on the nominal net worth. . . ."[20] The common stocks of 23 out of 44 consolidations were higher in price in 1914 than in 1900;[21] the common stocks of 21 were lower.

The Conference Board also gives figures through 1927 for a varying number of consolidations and points out that "Like other enterprises some go down in times of business stress, nor do all profit in equal degree from periods of business prosperity. Whether or not they have been more successful or less successful than enterprises organized upon a different basis there is no satisfactory means of measuring by statistical methods. But it at least seems to be clear that there are no inherent advantages in the consolidated form of organization

18. *Ibid.*, p. 94.
19. For the period 1904–1910, 48 consolidations were covered.
20. *Op. cit.*, p. 39.
21. Or the first year after 1900 for which prices were obtainable.

which insure greater profitableness for the investor than is offered by many non-consolidated enterprises."[22]

Shaw Livermore, however, disagrees with the above conclusions. His position is summarized in the following paragraph:

A reappraisal of the great merger era thus seems to be necessary, qualitatively as well as quantitatively. There was no general collapse of the companies which were formed; the percentage of those organized which have in a succeeding generation maintained records of earning power equal to or better than the standard for successful companies determined by Epstein is markedly higher than students of the period seem to have supposed. Once the initial decade of existence had passed, these surviving companies settled down to profitable careers—often as technical leaders in their respective fields. This ability to survive and attain success becomes more striking when mergers of lesser size and fame, neglected in previous analyses, are studied. The earning power which is the tangible measure of success has not been derived from excessive "watered" capitalization except in a small minority of cases. Nor was monopoly power, after the first decade, the means by which earnings were obtained. Business ability of a high order has emerged in the management of these once excoriated concerns, bringing them the earned respect of the business world. The existing estimate of them in economic literature would seem to require modification.[23]

B. 1909–1924

It has been shown that the majority[24] of large corporations

---

22. *Op. cit.*, pp. 85–86.
23. "The Success of Industrial Mergers," *The Quarterly Journal of Economics*, November 1935, pp. 68–96. The quotation is from pp. 89–90.
24. Based on 109 companies—the 93 that were in existence in 1914 plus the 16 that had failed prior to that year.

existing between 1900 and 1903 had, up to 1914, not been profitable for the investors who bought their common stocks, although some were exceptionally profitable. The outbreak of the war in 1914 was a windfall for most kinds of American businesses, especially those with war orders. Rising prices created opportunities for large profits. Furthermore, the higher price level raised the reproduction value of industrial plants and squeezed the water out of many a capital structure which before that time had been water-logged. The post-war reaction, marked by the depression of 1920–1921, caused considerable damage, but, on the whole, it did not seriously weaken the structure of American business. It should be noted, however, that war prosperity was not equally distributed among all branches of economic activity. Railroads and street railways, for example, were decided exceptions.

What happened to the 200 corporations which in 1909, a year of normal business, had the greatest amount of stocks and bonds outstanding?[25] What happened to them between that year and 1924—long enough after the war to justify the belief that business in general had got back to a normal peace-time condition?

Sixty-Three Per Cent of the Railroads Unprofitable

Of the 46 railroads in the list of 200 largest corporations at the end of 1909, 14 dropped out before the end of 1924. Of these, 12 went into receivership, one was acquired by a foreign corporation after a career of mediocre profits, and

25. Excluding all corporations of which a majority of the voting stock was owned by another corporation in the list of 200.

one, a holding company, disposed of its rail holdings at a loss and went out of business. Among the 32 which remained on the list not more than 17 were profitable investments.

One-Half of the Utilities and One-Fourth of the Industrials Unprofitable

Of the 55 utilities included among the 200 largest corporations at the end of 1909, 28 disappeared from the roster before the end of 1924. Receiverships and reorganizations claimed 12; 4, after several unprofitable years, were swallowed up in mergers; 2, though maintaining their existence, paid inadequate dividends and their stocks fell greatly in market value; 2 others seem to have been failures, although little information about them is available; 8 were moderately successful, but did not grow rapidly enough to stay among the 200. The 27 corporations which remained among the largest included 2 that paid no dividends on their common stock and practically none on their preferred, and 4 others whose stock was worth considerably less in 1924 than in 1909.[26] On the other hand, 8 were strikingly profitable to the owners of the common stocks because of the rise of 100 per cent or more in the market value of these shares.

Of 99 industrials included in the list of the 200 largest corporations at the end of 1909, 47 dropped out before the end of 1924. Seven of these dissolved or went into receivership, or entered into mergers on terms involving a loss of part of their original capital; 3 more had to write down their capi-

26. Allowing for exchanges, split-ups, stock dividends, changes in par value, etc.

tal; 9 were unable to pay their preferred dividends in full; and 2 others paid no common dividends during the 15 years. Ten merged or reorganized without loss, and 16 continued in existence although not growing rapidly enough to remain on the list. Taking into account dividends paid and changes in market value, not more than 24 of these 47 corporations were even moderately successful.

Fifty-two industrials remained on the list, but 2 of these were unable to pay their preferred dividends after 1921 and their stocks fell greatly in value between 1909 and 1924. Of the entire 99 industrials, not more than 74 were successful enough to make their common stocks good investments. In 40 instances, however, the common stock rose more than 100 per cent in value. There was a more than tenfold increase in the price of American Can Company stock, and nearly a sevenfold increase in the price of that of Corn Products Refining Company.

The 200 Giant Corporations as a Whole

Only about 120 of the 200 giant corporations of 1909 proved profitable for the investors in their common stocks over the following fifteen-year period, but 48 of them were very profitable. It is likely, however, that the capital lost in the unsuccessful stocks amounted to a larger sum than the capital gains and dividends received from the successful ones.

For only 161 of the 200 corporations was it possible to obtain information which showed the results of an investment in their common stocks. Assuming that 100 shares of each were bought in 1909 at the average price of that year, and sold in

1924 at the then average price, the investor would have received dividends averaging less than 6 per cent, probably considerably less, and would also have made a profit of 4.9 per cent over the entire fifteen-year period, or at the rate of a little less than one-third of 1 per cent per annum. He would have taken a large loss in 37 railroad stocks and a small loss in 42 utilities, but his gain from 82 industrials would have more than made up for these losses.

The nominal capitalization of the 200 giant corporations rose at the rate of 3.5 per cent a year between 1909 and 1924, while the national wealth rose at the rate of 5.1 per cent,[27] the national income at the rate of 6.6 per cent,[28] workingmen's weekly earnings at the rate of 5.9 per cent, the cost of living at the rate of 4.3 per cent and the general price level at the rate of 3.9 per cent.[29] Thus it would seem that the capitalization and the market value of the securities of large corporations grew more slowly in value than many other forms of wealth and sources of income.

C. 1919–1934

The "New Era," which ended in 1929, is generally regarded as a period in which corporations, especially the large ones, made huge profits. To some extent this impression is justified, but profits were not as great as stock prices indicated. Further-

27. Computed from data in Robert R. Doane, *The Measurement of American Wealth*, p. 11.

28. Computed from data in Willford Isbell King, *The National Income and Its Purchasing Power*, p. 74.

29. Computed from data in *Review of Economic Statistics*, February 15, 1934, p. 27.

more, they were largely offset by losses during the depression which followed the boom.

Earnings of Industrials and Utilities

The rates of net earnings[30] on total capitalization and also on common stock and surplus are shown in Table 28 for 40 industrials and 9 utilities, for the years from 1919 through 1934.[31] Railroads have been omitted because, on the whole, they suffered losses on their common stock equity, and made only slight profits on their total capitalization. The corporations analyzed were all among the 200 largest in the country in 1919. They were chosen as far as possible because they were either the ones that were appraised by the stock market as the most profitable, or the ones that were supposed to be most clearly monopolistic. The results shown in Table 28 are expressed both as arithmetic averages and as medians, the latter

30. Adjusted where "hidden" depreciation, obsolescence, profits or losses were discovered.

31. Industrials: American Can; American Sugar Refining; American Tobacco; Armour & Company (Illinois); Atlantic Refining; Bethlehem Steel; Corn Products Refining; Cuba Cane Sugar (Cuban Cane Products, 1930); Deere; du Pont; Eastman Kodak; General Electric; General Motors; International Harvester; Liggett & Myers Tobacco; P. Lorillard; National Biscuit; Ohio Oil; Pittsburgh Plate Glass; Prairie Oil and Gas; Prairie Pipe Line (Consolidated Oil, 1932); Procter & Gamble; Pullman; Quaker Oats; Republic Iron and Steel (Republic Steel, 1930); R. J. Reynolds Tobacco; Sears, Roebuck; Singer Manufacturing; Standard Oil (California); Standard Oil (Indiana); Standard Oil (New Jersey); Standard Oil (New York); Swift; United Fruit; United Shoe Machinery; United States Smelting, Refining and Mining; United States Steel; Vacuum Oil (Socony-Vacuum Oil, 1931); Wilson; F. W. Woolworth.

Public Utilities: American Gas and Electric; American Water Works and Electric; Brooklyn Union Gas; Columbia Gas and Electric; Consolidated Gas (New York); Consolidated Gas (Baltimore); North American; Pacific Lighting; Public Service (New Jersey).

TABLE 28

EARNINGS OF LARGE CORPORATIONS, 1919–1934[a]

Year	Forty Industrials				Nine Public Utilities			
	Per Cent on Total Capitalization		Per Cent on Common Stock and Surplus		Per Cent on Total Capitalization		Per Cent on Common Stock and Surplus	
	Arithmetic Average	Median	Arithmetic Average	Median	Arithmetic Average	Median	Arithmetic Average	Median
1919	11.9	9.6	12.7	11.4	4.8	4.3	5.7	4.1
1920	10.4	9.0	9.7	9.9	5.3	5.7	5.3	6.7
1921	4.3	4.3	1.5	4.1	4.9	5.2	6.0	5.6
1922	9.3	9.3	9.1	9.9	7.7	7.9	13.1	12.7
1923	9.9	9.0	10.0	9.6	7.7	7.8	11.5	10.2
1924	9.2	8.9	8.9	8.9	8.0	7.7	14.4	11.5
1925	10.5	11.5	9.8	11.9	7.9	8.0	15.5	11.4
1926	12.4	10.7	13.2	11.5	11.6	8.8	18.9	14.6
1927	11.4	9.5	11.6	10.0	9.9	7.8	19.9	9.1
1928	11.6	11.6	12.0	12.4	8.2	7.9	13.1	11.7
1929	11.4	10.3	11.3	11.4	7.5	7.7	11.8	11.4
1930	7.8	8.6	7.3	8.8	7.8	7.9	11.5	9.4
1931	6.0	5.7	4.5	3.3	6.4	6.4	8.3	8.7
1932	1.4	2.6	0.9	1.7	4.9	6.2	3.0	6.9
1933	3.3	5.0	1.3	5.6	5.5	5.9	4.9	6.1
1934	4.9	6.4	3.1	5.8	4.6	5.0	3.5	4.2
1919–1929b	10.2	9.5	10.0	10.0	7.6	7.8	12.3	11.4
1919–1934b	8.5	9.0	7.9	9.7	7.0	7.7	10.4	9.2

a. Computed from data published in various financial manuals.
b. Figures are the averages or medians of the annual figures.

in order to minimize the effect of a few extreme cases.

There was a sharp drop in the profits of industrial enterprises in 1921, followed by a sharp recovery in 1922. Then came a fairly steady rise through 1926, a slight decline in 1927, and a renewed up swing in 1928. A precipitous decline came in 1930, a further drop in 1931, and then a plunge to the bottom in 1932. There was a well marked recovery in 1933 and 1934. Except in a few years, earnings on total capitalization and on common stock and surplus did not differ greatly.

Earnings of utilities were low in 1919, and the 1921 depression had, therefore, only a very slight effect on them. The year 1922 brought a large increase in earnings, especially when profits are computed on common stock and surplus. The trend was mildly upward through 1926 or 1927, and then for three or four years it was mildly downward. The depression did not hit the utilities until 1931, but the downward trend had not been arrested as late as 1934.

Results for Entire Period

For the entire 16 years of good and bad business combined, the industrials earned, on the average, at the rate of 8.5 per cent or 9 per cent on total capital, and at the average rate of 7.9 per cent or 9.7 per cent on common stock and surplus; the utilities earned at the average rate of 7 per cent or 7.7 per cent on total capital, and at the average rate of 10.4 per cent or 9.2 per cent on common stock and surplus.[32] The rates are surprisingly little higher when the depression years of 1930 to

32. In each case, the first figure is the arithmetic average; the second, the median.

1934 are eliminated, especially when they are computed on total capitalization.

Wide Differences Among Companies

The individual companies show an extremely wide range of average earnings over the sixteen-year period. The R. J. Reynolds Tobacco Company led the industrials with profits of 19.9 per cent on common stock and surplus. The Eastman Kodak Company, General Motors Corporation and F. W. Woolworth Company each earned between 17 and 18 per cent. At the bottom of the list were five companies that had deficits: Armour and Company of Illinois (6.4 per cent); Cuba Cane Sugar Company (12.2 per cent); Deere and Company (1.5 per cent); Republic Iron and Steel Company (1.6 per cent); and Wilson and Company (8.0 per cent). Six other companies earned less than 5 per cent on their common stock and surplus.

Each of the nine utilities made money, and each averaged more than 6 per cent. The American Gas and Electric Company had the best results—20.1 per cent. Consolidated Gas Company of New York[33] was at the bottom of the list with profits of 6.9 per cent on common stock and surplus.

Profits of Investors in 191 Common Stocks

A study was made of the income and profits of investors who purchased the common stocks of 191 corporations at the average prices in 1919 and sold them at the average prices either in 1929 or 1934.[34] The total of 191 corporations in-

33. Now the Consolidated Edison Company.
34. Cash dividends and salable rights have been treated as current in-

cludes 115 industrials, 35 public utilities and 41 railroads.
The returns to investors before 1929 were at a much higher
rate than the profits of the corporations in which they invested; but after 1929 they were at a much lower rate. It was
the profits of investors that made the "New Era" seem so
prosperous.

Detailed figures, not presented in the text, show that cheap
railroad shares were better investments than cheap industrials,
but that higher priced railroad shares were not as good as the
higher priced industrials. Utility stocks were much better investments than either rails or industrials.

Individual stocks varied enormously. The best investment
on the list was the Toledo, St. Louis and Western Railroad
(93.7 per cent per annum), followed by the American Can
Company (40.8 per cent).[35] Four utilities, 19 railroads and
53 industrials—a total of 76 out of 191—were losing investments over the fifteen-year period. Even during the prosperous
decade, 1919–1929, there were 34 losing investments—1
utility, 2 rails and 31 industrials.

The appreciation in market value of the industrials from
1919 to 1929 was at the average annual rate of 3 per cent,
assuming an equal amount of cash invested in each corporation. If 100 shares of each had been purchased, the appreciation would have been 10.5 per cent. The annual rate of appreciation of the median corporation was 4.6 per cent. In

come. Stock dividends have been added to the investment and the price per
share adjusted to allow for them. The average annual rate of current income is
a simple arithmetic average of the total received in the years under discussion.
Price appreciation, however, has been computed like compound interest.
35. Cash income and appreciation combined.

TABLE 29

RESULTS OF INVESTMENTS IN COMMON STOCKS IN 1919[a]

		Average Rate of Return		
		A	B	C
115 Industrials				
Current income	1919–1929	6.4	6.6	5.5
	1919–1934	6.3	6.6	5.1
Appreciation	1919–1929	3.0	10.5	4.6
	1919–1934	–4.9	1.5	–3.3
Appreciation and income	1919–1929	9.4	17.1	5.4
	1919–1934	1.4	8.1	0.9
35 Public Utilities				
Current income	1919–1929	10.3	9.8	9.7
	1919–1934	10.8	10.4	9.5
Appreciation	1919–1929	15.6	20.7	13.1
	1919–1934	–2.1	2.4	–1.0
Appreciation and income	1919–1929	25.8	30.4	23.9
	1919–1934	8.7	12.8	9.1
41 Railroads				
Current income	1919–1929	9.0	7.8	7.8
	1919–1934	8.8	6.9	6.6
Appreciation	1919–1929	7.4	1.0	10.1
	1919–1934	–3.6	–2.0	–4.2
Appreciation and income	1919–1929	16.4	8.9	14.6
	1919–1934	5.2	4.9	1.3
191 Stocks				
Current income	1919–1929	7.7	7.1	6.9
	1919–1934	7.6	7.0	6.3
Appreciation	1919–1929	6.2	11.8	7.7
	1919–1934	–4.1	1.4	–3.3
Appreciation and income	1919–1929	13.9	18.9	14.6
	1919–1934	3.5	8.4	1.7

LEGEND: A = Average: equal amount invested in each corporation.
 B = Average: equal number of shares bought in each corporation.
 C = Median corporation.

a. Computed from data published in various financial manuals. Minus signs indicate depreciation.

addition, cash dividends and salable rights averaged 6.4 per cent or 6.6 per cent a year, with a median of 5.5 per cent.

The depression reduced the average appreciation of the 1919–1934 period to 1.5 per cent, on the assumption of an original investment in 100 shares of each industrial corporation. On the assumption of an equal cash investment in each company, there was no appreciation but, instead, an average annual depreciation of 4.9 per cent. The median stock depreciated 3.3 per cent per year. The average annual cash yield was 6.3 per cent or 6.6 per cent, and the median yield 5.1 per cent.

This information is summarized in Table 29, together with corresponding figures for rails and utilities.

Chapter 11

PROFITS AND DIVIDENDS OF FOUR HUNDRED AND FIFTY LEADING INDUSTRIAL, UTILITY AND RAILROAD CORPORATIONS, 1927–1935

THE STANDARD Statistics Company, Inc. has tabulated the important income-account and balance-sheet items of 450 leading industrial, utility and railroad corporations for each year from 1927 through 1935. The data do not permit conclusions as to the relationship between size and profits, for the corporations are classified by industry and not by size.[1] They are, however, valuable for the purpose of showing changes from year to year and differences among industrial groups. They cover a period of nine years, characterized by prosperity, depression and recovery, and they represent identical corporations in each group in each year.

In the analysis that follows, only three items will be discussed: net profit,[2] which is the term used by the Standard

1. The average assets of each group and sub-group can be computed, but since each group consists of corporations of various sizes this is not very helpful. The average assets of the three principal economic divisions in 1935 were: industrials, $66.3 million; utilities, $427.4 million; railroads, $616.2 million. Obviously, the tabulation covers groups of corporations that, on the whole, are well up in the giant class. The utilities and the railroads are, indeed, super-giants.

2. "Net profit," as used by the Standard Statistics Company, is, roughly, the equivalent of "total profit," as used in Chapter 6 of this volume.

123

Statistics Company to indicate the amount available for fixed charges; net income, which is the amount available for dividends; and cash dividends paid on the outstanding common stock. These are presented in Table 30 in the form of index numbers, in order to facilitate year-to-year comparisons.

TABLE 30

CHANGES IN NET PROFIT, NET INCOME AND COMMON STOCK
DIVIDENDS OF 450 CORPORATIONS, BY PRINCIPAL
ECONOMIC GROUPS, 1927–1935[a]

(*Index Numbers;* 1928 = 100)

	1927	1928	1929	1930	1931	1932	1933	1934	1935
				403 Industrials					
Net profit	77	100	113	68	29	9	28	39	56
Net income	75	100	114	66	24	3	24	36	54
Common dividends	89	100	117	112	88	53	42	52	60
				22 Utilities					
Net profit	85	100	112	115	112	98	92	84	88
Net income	82	100	115	119	112	85	74	67	75
Common dividends	80	100	117	147	152	131	105	92	84
				25 Railroads					
Net profit	95	100	111	88	60	44	50	49	50
Net income	92	100	120	76	26	−2	8	8	10
Common dividends	93	100	108	114	79	23	22	29	29

a. Standard Statistics Company, Inc., *Composite of Financial Statements,* August 14, 1936, p. 2. The minus sign indicates a deficit expressed as a percentage of the 1928 net income. For definition of "net profit" see footnote 2, p. 123.

Earnings of Industrials, Rails and Utilities

The peak of net profit[3] and of net income came in 1929 for industrials and railroads, but not until 1930 for utilities. The

3. See footnote 2, p. 123.

bottom of the down swing was reached in 1932 by the industrials and rails, but not until 1934 by the utilities.

Utilities suffered relatively little from the depression. Their earnings available for fixed charges (i.e., net profit) registered a maximum decline of only 16 per cent from 1928, and even their net income available for dividends fell off only 33 per cent. As against this, the net profit of the industrials declined 91 per cent from 1928 to 1932, and their net income 97 per cent. During the same interval, the net profit of the rails declined less than that of the industrials—56 per cent—but their net income disappeared entirely and became a small deficit. After 1932, the industrials recovered sharply but the rails staged only a slight comeback. The utilities made a small gain in their first year of recovery.

Dividend Payments

The common stock dividend payments of the industrials reached a high point in 1929 and fell steadily thereafter through 1933, in which year they were 58 per cent less than in 1928. They rose appreciably in 1934 and made a further gain in 1935.

The dividend payments of the railroads, on the other hand, were larger in 1930 than in 1929, but once they started to decline, they fell off much more sharply than did industrial dividends. They reached their low in 1933—78 per cent off from 1928. They had a fair rise in 1934, but showed no further improvement in 1935.

Common dividends of utilities were much larger in 1930 than in 1929 and increased still further in 1931. Their decline did not start until 1932, but it continued through 1935. They remained above the 1928 level, however, until 1934, and even in 1935 were only 16 per cent below the base year, though 45 per cent below the peak year. The drop in industrial common stock dividends from their peak to 1935 was only slightly greater, namely 49 per cent, but the decline in railroad dividends from their high to their low amounted to 75 per cent.

Dividends held up better than earnings available for dividends in each of the three divisions.[4] The industrials had to dig into their surplus to meet dividend payments in 1931, 1932 and 1933; the rails, in every year covered beginning with 1931. The utilities, however, regularly met their dividend payments out of current earnings.

Earnings of Industrials by Groups

The tabulation of the Standard Statistics Company classifies the data for 403 industrial corporations in 28 principal groups.[5] Ten of the more important groups, embracing more than half of the total number of industrial corporations, are covered by Table 31, but only a few of the comparisons suggested by this table can be discussed in the text.

Textiles and apparel furnish an interesting contrast to tobacco and tobacco products. In the former group, net profit and net income started to decline as early as 1928[6] and con-

4. Except that the railroads increased their net income more than their dividend payments between 1928 and 1929.
5. Several of the groups are further subdivided. There is also an aircraft group, but it is not included in the summary as data on it are not available prior to 1933.
6. Earnings started to decline in the automobile industry in 1929.

tinued to decline drastically through 1932, in which year the industry failed to meet even its fixed charges. Tobacco, on the other hand, showed an increasing net profit and net income each year through 1931, and only a small decline in 1932. In 1933, however, earnings in the textile industry turned sharply upward, while those in tobacco fell appreciably. But in 1934, tobacco registered recovery while the textile industry lost nearly half of its previous year's gain. In 1935, there was again a deviation between the trends. Tobacco showed stationary earnings, but textile earnings improved markedly.

Steel the Most Erratic Performer

Steel and iron was the most erratic performer of any group covered. The earnings made a bigger gain than any other in the boom year 1929—55 per cent over 1928 in net profit and 70 per cent in net income—but next to textiles and apparel they showed the largest falling off between 1928 and 1932. Only two of the industries failed to meet fixed charges in 1933. Steel was one of them—and the one to fail by the larger margin. Machinery was the other. Steel was the only industry that had a deficit in 1934.

Against steel's erratic behavior may be contrasted the relatively even flow of earnings in the chemicals and fertilizer industry, in food products, in retail trade and, above all, in tobacco and tobacco products.

Recovery since 1932

Nineteen twenty-eight earnings were most closely approached in 1935 by the chemicals and fertilizer industry, but

TABLE 31

CHANGES IN NET PROFIT, NET INCOME AND COMMON STOCK DIVIDENDS OF 208 CORPORATIONS, BY INDUSTRIAL GROUPS, 1927–1935[a]

(*Index Numbers; 1928 = 100*)

Industrial Groups	Number of Corporations	Average Assets 1935 (Millions of Dollars)	Items	1927	1928	1929	1930	1931	1932	1933	1934	1935
Automobiles and trucks	13	123.88	Net profit[b]	79	100	89	43	22	−10	21	21	51
			Net income	79	100	89	42	21	−11	20	21	50
			Common dividends	81	100	100	81	70	30	27	32	48
Chemicals and fertilizer	19	81.54	Net profit	77	100	118	91	66	36	55	68	87
			Net income	76	100	119	91	66	35	54	68	87
			Common dividends	83	100	117	111	100	67	62	75	91
Electrical equipment and radio	10	68.77	Net profit	76	100	107	70	33	2	4	24	43
			Net income	76	100	106	70	32	0	4	23	43
			Common dividends	78	100	93	107	94	32	20	30	46
Food products	28	75.20	Net profit	80	100	112	105	64	46	66	67	69
			Net income	76	100	114	106	59	40	64	66	69
			Common dividends	92	100	117	135	132	108	75	92	90
Machinery (industrial and agricultural)	24	41.51	Net profit	84	100	132	89	6	−32	−8	22	62
			Net income	84	100	132	86	2	−37	−11	20	61
			Common dividends	83	100	121	128	97	47	43	52	62

TABLE 31 (Continued)

Industrial Groups	Number of Corporations	Average Assets 1935 (Millions of Dollars)	Items	1927	1928	1929	1930	1931	1932	1933	1934	1935
								Years				
Oil producing and refining	26	276.59	Net profit	53	100	112	58	-13	20	23	36	51
			Net income	50	100	113	53	-11	13	17	30	47
			Common dividends	102	100	132	129	87	62	42	51	49
Retail trade	25	52.50	Net profit	95	100	100	67	57	25	60	69	76
			Net income	96	100	100	65	55	21	57	67	75
			Common dividends	94	100	119	114	127	77	59	69	85
Steel and iron	18	190.34	Net profit	82	100	155	36	10	-47	-18	1	22
			Net income	78	100	170	87	-1	-69	-34	-10	14
			Common dividends	89	100	136	134	67	2	0	2	7
Textiles and apparel	29	14.15	Net profit	116	100	96	2	-21	-78	71	5	43
			Net income	117	100	98	-6	-29	-90	78	4	46
			Common dividends	141	100	145	130	99	48	35	63	65
Tobacco and tobacco products	16	51.20	Net profit	97	100	110	123	126	115	70	84	85
			Net income	97	100	110	124	128	118	71	86	86
			Common dividends	94	100	110	131	131	130	126	134	124

a. Computed from data in Standard Statistics Company, Inc., op. cit., pp. 6-7, 10-15, 18-19, 22-31. Minus signs indicate deficits expressed as percentages of the 1928 income.

b. For definition of "net profit," see footnote 2, p. 123.

tobacco and tobacco products was very little behind. The next best showing was made by retail trade. Steel and iron made the poorest showing, with electrical equipment and textiles next. Automobiles and trucks had higher earnings in 1935 than in 1930, as did retail trade and textiles and apparel. Net profit and net income were higher in 1935 than in 1931 in each industrial group except tobacco and tobacco products.

Dividends

Dividend disbursements were larger in 1928 than in 1927 in each industrial group except oil producing and refining and textiles and apparel. A further increase took place in 1929, except in automobiles and trucks, where there was no change, and in electrical equipment and radio, where there was a 7 per cent decline. Four industrial groups increased common dividend payments in 1930; six reduced them. Only one industry—retail trade—paid more in 1931 than in 1930. Tobacco and tobacco products paid the same amount in the two years. Each of the ten groups cut dividend payments on their common stocks in 1932, and cut them still further in 1933, although earnings had already started to improve. All groups increased their disbursements in 1934, and seven of them increased them still further in 1935. The three exceptions were food, oil and tobacco.

Stockholders Fared Worst in Steel; Best in Tobacco

During the four years beginning with 1932, the steel and iron industry paid virtually no common stock dividends. The tobacco industry, on the other hand, maintained its dividends throughout the depression at a level well above their 1929 payments. Stockholders in chemicals, food and retail trade suffered comparatively small reductions of income during the depression, but those in the automobile industry and in electrical equipment and radio were hard hit. Dividends were well sustained in textiles and apparel, in view of the unsatisfactory earning record of this industry.

Chapter 12

PROFITS AND DIVIDENDS OF SIX HUNDRED AND SEVENTY-SEVEN LARGE CORPORATIONS, 1928–1932

A TABULATION has been made[1] of the net income[2] and the combined common and preferred cash dividends of 677 corporations for each year from 1928 through 1932. The data are classified in four assets classes and twenty industrial groups and sub-groups, as shown in Table 32.

Changes in Net Income and Dividends

The changes in net income and in dividends paid are given in the form of index numbers in Table 33 for all corporations classified by size.

Three of the four classes increased net incomes between 1928 and 1929, the exception being the $5 million-to-$10 million class. The biggest increase came in the biggest class. This class also made the best record when the effects of the depression are measured. Between 1928 and 1932 its net income declined 84 per cent, as against declines of 95 and 94 per cent in the smallest two classes. The second largest class

---

1. From data published in financial manuals.
2. Available for dividends.

TABLE 32

DISTRIBUTION OF 677 CORPORATIONS, BY INDUSTRIAL GROUPS AND BY ASSETS CLASSES

(Total Assets Classes in Thousands of Dollars)

Industrial Groups	Number of Corporations				
		Total Assets Classes			
	Total	1,000–5,000	5,000–10,000	10,000–50,000	50,000 and Over
Agriculture	2	–	–	1	1
Mining	64	15	10	21	18
Total manufacturing	454	80	80	205	89
Food	54	11	8	26	9
Tobacco	18	3	3	8	4
Textiles	43	12	7	22	2
Chemicals	40	4	6	24	6
Petroleum	35	3	4	9	19
Iron and steel, excluding machinery	58	9	12	23	14
Machinery, excluding transportation equipment	41	6	6	22	7
Transportation equipment	47	8	8	20	11
Other manufacturing industries	118	24	26	51	17
Construction	11	1	3	6	1
Transportation and other public utilities	34	2	4	6	22
Electric light, power and gas	17	–	1	2	14
Trade, wholesale and retail	71	13	11	37	10
Retail trade	66	11	11	34	10
Service	21	3	3	11	4
Finance, including investment trust and security trading	20	2	3	13	2
Investment trust and security trading	13	1	2	9	1
All corporations	677	116	114	300	147

had a deficit in 1932 which was nearly one-sixth as large as its net income in 1928.

TABLE 33

Changes in Net Income and Dividends of 677 Corporations, by Assets Classes, 1928–1932[a]

(*Index Numbers;* 1928 = 100. *Total Assets Classes in Thousands of Dollars*)

Net Income and Dividends	Years	Total Assets Classes				
		Total	1,000– 5,000	5,000– 10,000	10,000– 50,000	50,000 and Over
Net Income	1928	100	100	100	100	100
	1929	122	110	98	114	126
	1930	72	53	46	57	79
	1931	28	27	14	20	30
	1932	9	5	6	–15	16
Dividends	1928	100	100	100	100	100
	1929	127	131	133	121	108
	1930	123	119	156	134	102
	1931	96	99	113	89	86
	1932	65	58	82	55	52

a. Minus sign indicates deficit expressed as percentage of the 1928 income.

In spite of the fact that the giant class had the best income record, it increased its dividends in 1929 by only 8 per cent, while the three other classes made increases of one-fifth to one-third. Then in the depression it reduced its dividends more than any of the other classes, though only slightly more than two of the others. The $5 million-to-$10 million class is conspicuous for the largeness of its dividend increases and the smallness of its dividend reductions. Even in the worst depression year it disbursed more than four-fifths as much as in 1928, while each of the three other classes disbursed less than three-fifths as much.

Variations Among Industries

Table 34 brings out the variations among the principal industrial groups for all size classes combined.

TABLE 34

CHANGES IN NET INCOME AND DIVIDENDS OF 677 CORPORATIONS, BY INDUSTRIAL GROUPS, 1928–1932[a]

(*Index Numbers; 1928 = 100*)

Industrial Groups	Net Income					Dividends				
	1928	1929	1930	1931	1932	1928	1929	1930	1931	1932
Agriculture	100	84	62	29	20	100	104	116	106	63
Mining	100	162	56	4	−17	100	717	427	181	49
Total manufacturing	100	123	68	15	0	100	121	119	94	58
Construction	100	115	71	30	6	100	123	138	111	55
Transportation and other public utilities	100	115	112	93	71	100	145	165	161	114
Trade	100	105	63	50	16	100	122	122	126	76
Service	100	125	27	−23	−114	100	108	362	132	56
Finance	100	146	73	11	−40	100	150	158	115	59
All corporations	100	122	72	29	9	100	127	123	96	65

a. Minus signs indicate deficits expressed as percentages of the 1928 income.

Of the eight principal groups, mining made the greatest gain in net income—62 per cent—when 1929 is compared with 1928. Except for agriculture, which showed a decline,[3]

3. The sample of agricultural corporations is, however, too small to be trustworthy.

trade was at the bottom of the list, with a gain of only 5 per cent. There was a falling off in 1930 in each group. It was sharpest in service and almost negligible in transportation and other public utilities. The last named group was the only one whose net income was higher in 1930 than in 1928. Further declines took place in 1931. They were moderate in transportation and other public utilities and in trade, but virtually wiped out the net income of mining concerns and placed service "in the red." In 1932, the index was at the bottom in each group. Mining, service and finance showed deficits. The service corporations had a deficit greater than their profit of 1928. Transportation and other public utilities, on the other hand, still showed a net income that was within striking distance of the 1928 figure.

Dividends held up much better than income. In five of the eight industrial groups the peak was not reached until 1930, and in trade not until 1931. In transportation and other public utilities dividend payments were higher in 1932 than in 1928. Mining companies showed by far the most violent fluctuations of any group. In 1929 their dividends were more than seven times as high as in 1928. Each year thereafter they dropped precipitously, until in 1932 they stood at slightly less than half the 1928 level. Next to transportation and other public utilities, trade was the group in which dividends were best maintained during the depression. These were the two groups which were also most successful in maintaining net income.[4]

4. Because of the inadequacy of the sample, agriculture was left out of consideration.

Industrial Differences Among Assets Classes

The preceding section compared industries as a whole. Further differences appear when the groups are compared as to the relationship of the assets classes within each. This is brought out in Table 35 for the three main groups and the three manufacturing sub-groups, which have sufficient representation in each assets class to justify conclusions.

The smallest assets class[5] made the best income showing in iron and steel and in transportation equipment. In both these groups it was the only class with a net income in 1932. Only in total manufacturing was the largest assets class at the top. In mining the smallest and largest classes showed the greatest falling off. The second smallest class had the poorest results in food products, transportation equipment and in trade, and the best results in no group. The second largest class did best of any in mining, food and in trade, and worst of any in total manufacturing and in iron and steel.

When 1928 is compared with 1932 as to dividends, differences again appear in each industrial group. Dividends were maintained best by the smallest assets class in total manufacturing, in iron and steel and in transportation equipment; by the second smallest class in trade; by the second largest class in mining and by the largest in food. On the other hand, the worst showing of any among the assets classes was made by the smallest class in food and trade; by the second smallest and second largest classes in manufacturing and by the largest in mining, iron and steel and transportation.

5. It should be remembered that in this chapter the smallest class consists of corporations with assets from $1 million to $5 million.

TABLE 35

CHANGES IN NET INCOME AND DIVIDENDS OF 589 CORPORATIONS, BY
INDUSTRIAL GROUPS AND BY ASSETS CLASSES, 1928–1932[a]

(Index Numbers; 1928 = 100. Total Assets Classes in Thousands of Dollars)

Industrial Groups	Years	Net Income — Total Assets Classes				Dividends — Total Assets Classes			
		1,000–5,000	5,000–10,000	10,000–50,000	50,000 and Over	1,000–5,000	5,000–10,000	10,000–50,000	50,000 and Over
Mining	1928	100	100	100	100	100	100	100	100
	1929	61	73	134	197	126	121	384	202
	1930	−2	29	73	60	65	174	319	112
	1931	−38	17	14	−1	32	60	218	46
	1932	−31	7	8	−31	17	60	191	5
Total manufacturing	1928	100	100	100	100	100	100	100	100
	1929	115	104	110	129	126	80	120	121
	1930	56	46	55	74	139	93	120	116
	1931	32	7	17	14	104	77	87	95
	1932	4	−3	−17	7	71	52	52	58
Food	1928	100	100	100	100	100	100	100	100
	1929	105	127	111	127	176	126	102	125
	1930	97	107	103	97	128	142	115	143
	1931	60	22	88	68	129	130	113	139
	1932	27	2	62	45	85	95	99	117
Iron and steel	1928	100	100	100	100	100	100	100	100
	1929	186	116	139	143	314	152	7	140
	1930	33	34	58	64	190	221	7	132
	1931	−21	−17	−19	−2	133	74	69	83
	1932	40	−25	−52	−25	52	30	32	29
Transportation equipment	1928	100	100	100	100	100	100	100	100
	1929	108	55	97	115	144	186	153	112
	1930	65	−16	16	43	95	113	161	86
	1931	33	−69	60	−32	140	44	111	53
	1932	9	−86	−80	−35	90	18	40	16
Trade	1928	100	100	100	100	100	100	100	100
	1929	96	108	116	99	90	183	109	126
	1930	51	74	62	63	139	201	135	121
	1931	22	46	57	47	120	159	100	138
	1932	10	−2	21	15	69	104	80	72

a. Minus signs indicate deficits expressed as percentages of the 1928 income.

PART FOUR

SUMMARY AND CONCLUSIONS

Chapter 13

SUMMARY

1. Findings of Preceding Volume of Series

About 57 per cent of all economic activity is incorporated, the range being from 6 per cent in agriculture to 96 per cent in mining and quarrying. Of 388,564 active corporations submitting balance sheets to the Bureau of Internal Revenue in 1933, there were 594 that had assets of at least $50 million each. This handful of giants owned 53 per cent of total corporate wealth. On the other hand, there were 211,586 small corporations, each with assets under $50,000. In the aggregate, they owned only 1.4 per cent of the corporate wealth.

There was also a pronounced concentration of corporate income. Thirty-six per cent went to the giant corporations, while the large number of corporations with assets of less than $50,000 each, received but 2.2 per cent.[1]

When all American economic activity is considered—that part which is not incorporated as well as that part which is— the position of the giant corporations becomes less conspicuous, though still remaining prominent. In 1933, the 594 largest corporations accounted for 18.4 per cent of the total national income produced, government included; or for 20 per cent, government excluded.

1. I.e., statutory net income.

141

2. The Measurement of Profits

Profits can be measured by numerous standards. Two of them were applied in the text[2] to data from *Statistics of Income*—the ratio of net income to net worth and the ratio of total profit to total capitalization.[3] These standards were used to study the relationship between size and profitableness.

The possible presence of "water" in capital structures was disregarded because it would not affect the conclusion of the analyses to any appreciable extent. The rise of prices caused by the World War soaked up much of the water that had previously been present. There are no doubt still many corporations whose assets are overvalued in their balance sheets, but they are to at least some extent offset by other corporations whose assets are undervalued. Furthermore, when comparisons are made between classes of corporations, the existence of water is not a material factor unless it occurs in one class to a greater degree than in another. There is no proof that it does.

Although stock dividends and "split-ups" are sometimes thought to be the causes of watered capitalization, this should not be charged against them. They may bring about inflation of the market prices of securities, but they cannot inflate the value of corporate assets or increase the book value of net worth.

Aside from the question of water, the validity of the analysis of *Statistics of Income* is subject to some doubt because of the shortcomings of the underlying data. The figures cover three

2. Two additional standards are presented in Appendices D and E.
3. These terms are explained on pp. 9–10 and also in the Glossary.

years only, all of which were years of serious depression. The assets classes in which the corporations are classified are of very unequal range. Furthermore, they do not cover identical corporations each year. The industrial groups are too broad, and are not equally represented in the various assets classes. Finally, the data are summations of hundreds of thousands of separate corporate income-tax returns which are themselves not homogeneous. The conclusions that have been reached must, therefore, be regarded as tentative.

The data underlying the analysis of specific groups of large corporations in Part Three extend over longer periods of time and cover identical corporations within each group from year to year. Their principal shortcomings are that they apply only to the larger corporations and that they are only small samples of even this small class. The outstanding advantage of the income-tax statistics is their extensive coverage.

3. GROSS INCOME AND TOTAL COSTS

There seems to be no definite relationship between size and changes in gross income or changes in total costs. Among all corporations, however, the largest assets class showed greater declines in both gross income and total costs from 1931 to 1932 than any other class and the least recovery from 1932 to 1933.

All corporations, and profitable corporations by themselves, exhibit a well defined tendency for the ratio of costs to income to grow more favorable with increasing assets size. In addition, the ratios of costs to income were most favorable in the largest assets class in each of the three groups in each year, with the exception of the group of profitable corporations in 1933 when the $10 million-to-$50 million class had the lead. For example, among all corporations in 1933, the total costs of the smallest class were 5.5 per cent in excess of their gross income. In the median class, the excess of costs was only 1.9 per cent. In the largest class, income was 2.7 per cent greater than costs.

There is no clear trend in the unprofitable group, but in this group, too, the largest corporations had the best ratios.

All assets classes in all three groups, but above all in the profitable one, made close adjustments of costs to changes in gross income.[4] For instance, the income of giant corporations as a whole declined 22 per cent between 1931 and 1933, while their costs decreased 20.4 per cent.

There are variations among industries as to changes in gross income and total costs, and as to the ratio of costs to income. An interesting fact is that the largest class of financial corporations earned the largest percentage of profit on gross income of any of the giants in the six industrial groups and subgroups studied. But among the same groups of corporations in the smallest assets class, the financial concerns suffered the largest percentage of loss.

4. The Relationship Between Size and Profits Before 1931

Prior to 1931, only scattered and incomplete data on the

---

4. The poorest adjustment appears in the all-corporations group in respect to changes between 1932 and 1933.

relationship between size and profits were published in *Statistics of Income.*

Figures for 1919 show that the ratio of net income to invested capital declined almost uninterruptedly from 27.8 per cent in the smallest invested capital class to 9.7 per cent in the largest.

Figures on consolidated returns from 1928 through 1933 prove that corporations using this form of return were, on the whole, very much larger than the others, and that they suffered more severely during the depression. But since corporations of all sizes make consolidated returns, precise conclusions as to the relationship between size and profits cannot be drawn.

5. Net Income on Net Worth

When profit is defined as the ratio of net income to net worth, it is found that the large corporations that made profits made them at lower rates than the small ones, while the large corporations that lost money lost at lower rates than the small ones. There is, however, a much more clearly defined trend in the profitable than in the unprofitable group. The trend line for all corporations closely resembles that for unprofitable corporations. Among profitable corporations, the smallest class showed the largest profit ratio in each year; the largest class, the smallest in two of the three years. In the unprofitable group the smallest corporations showed the largest loss ratio in each year, while the giants showed the smallest. To illustrate, in 1933 the smallest class of profitable corporations made a profit of 8.6 per cent, while the largest class made a profit of only 4.7 per cent. The smallest class of unprofitable corporations, however, had a loss of 37.8 per cent, against a loss of only 2 per cent for the giants.

The only class that shows a net income when the profitable and unprofitable corporations are combined, is the largest. This class made a profit in each of the years covered. Of the 594 giants of 1933, however, only 200 were profitable; and in each of the two other years as well, only a minority of the giants made money.

Year-to-year comparisons indicate that 1932 was a poorer year than 1931, and that 1933 was better than 1932. On the whole, 1933 was better than 1931 for the unprofitable corporations and worse for the profitable ones.

Changes between years were smaller in the profitable group than in the unprofitable. The business recovery in 1933 is more clearly reflected in the results of the unprofitable corporations than of the profitable ones, but this merely means that the unprofitable corporations had more room for improvement.

A breakdown of the figures into industrial groups and sub-groups brings to light many significant variations among profitable corporations and also among profitable and unprofitable corporations combined. Transportation and other public utilities, for instance, showed a slight profit in 1932, although all industries combined had a loss in that year. Manufacturing as a whole lost money, but tobacco companies were very profitable. The food products and chemical industries were also "in the black"—by slight margins. Furthermore there were many deviations from the profit trend for all industries. Among profitable trade corporations, for example, it was the largest and not the smallest class that showed the highest rate of profit.

In the unprofitable group, there were few and only unimportant variations from the trend for the unprofitable corporations in all industries combined.

6. Total Profit on Total Capitalization

The ratio of total profit to total capitalization brings out much the same relationship among the assets classes as does the ratio of net income to net worth. There is the same general tendency for the rate of profit of profitable corporations, and the rate of deficit of unprofitable corporations, to grow smaller as the assets classes increase. The principal result of adding interest paid to net income and borrowed capital to net worth, is that, on the whole, the profitable corporations earn smaller profits and the unprofitable corporations incur smaller losses than they do without these additions.

When the overall figures are broken down by industries, variations among the groups are brought to light—as always.

When comparisons of the ratios of total profit to total capitalization are made between years, it appears that, with a few exceptions, results were less favorable in 1932 than in 1931 and more favorable in 1933 than in 1932. They were, in general, more favorable in 1933 than in 1931, except among profitable corporations.

That the profit ratios change when consideration is given to borrowed capital and interest paid, indicates that there must be differences in the capital structures of the separate classes.

The facts are that the larger corporations get a larger proportion of their capital from stockholders and a smaller proportion from lenders than the smaller ones. Furthermore, the fixed portion of the borrowed capital increases, and the floating portion decreases, as the assets classes increase in size. Because of these two factors, larger corporations are safer than smaller ones, especially during a depression.

7. The Influence of Turnover on Rate of Profit

It was shown in Chapters 5 and 6 that the rate of profit on capital decreases with increasing assets size, and that the rate of deficit also decreases with increasing size. These facts cannot be accounted for by the trend of the ratio of net income to gross income.

The relationship between size and turnover of capital does, however, offer an explanation. The rate of turnover decreases steadily with increasing size. This is true of profitable and of unprofitable corporations, and of all industrial groups studied, except finance. For this reason any given rate of profit or deficit on gross income becomes a larger rate of profit or deficit on the capital of small corporations, and becomes a smaller rate of profit or deficit on the capital of large ones.

8. Dividends

When all corporations are considered, the smallest five classes, on the whole, reduced dividend payments by greater percentages than the next three larger ones. The giant class, however, made the third largest reduction between 1931 and

1932, the second largest between 1932 and 1933 and the very largest between 1931 and 1933. The $10 million-to-$50 million class had the best record.

Among profitable corporations, there is a clear trend for dividend changes between 1931 and 1932 to become increasingly less favorable with increasing assets size. The 1932–1933 changes, however, reveal the opposite trend. No trend is discernible between 1931 and 1933.

No definite trends appear in the unprofitable group. On the whole, however, the largest corporations made the biggest reductions.

The sample analysis of six industrial groups and sub-groups shows slight variations in the largest assets class, but appreciable ones in the smallest class.

More important than dividend changes is the percentage of net income disbursed as dividends. In the case of profitable corporations the percentage rises steadily with increasing assets size, with only two unimportant breaks. The largest corporations distributed more than they earned in each year. Unprofitable corporations show a similar trend in terms of minus ratios.

Among the industrial groups studied no relationship can be seen in finance between size and the ratio of dividends to profits. The ratios of the other groups, however, followed the trend shown by all industries. Chemicals and allied products show the highest ratios, for industries as a whole, in 1931 and 1932; transportation and other public utilities, in 1933. The ratio was lowest in finance in all three years.

The tendency of the ratio of dividends to net income to increase with increasing assets size can best be explained by the fact that surplus and undivided profits become an increasingly larger percentage of total capitalization as the assets classes increase.

When the ratio of dividends to the stockholders' equity are considered, it is found that, on the whole, the larger corporations paid larger dividends in relation to their net worth than the smaller ones. There are, however, many breaks in the trend, especially in the smallest classes. The giant class paid the largest percentage on net worth in 1931 and 1932, and the second largest in 1933.

The ratio of common dividends to common stock shows an even more pronounced trend of increasing ratios with increasing assets size than that of the ratio of total dividends to net worth.

Except finance, the individual industries show, in general, similar trends to that for all industries. The trends, however, are in some cases more irregular. In finance, the largest ratio of dividends to net worth occurs in the smallest, or second smallest, class.

The chemical industry displays the highest ratio under all returns; transportation and other public utilities, under profitable corporations; finance, under unprofitable corporations. The metal industry displays the lowest ratios under all returns and under unprofitable corporations; trade and finance under profitable corporations.

9. Special Consideration of Banking Profits

Commercial banking operations were fairly profitable during the first two decades of the century, the decline which had set in immediately prior to the outbreak of war in Europe being followed by a reverse movement as the result of war prosperity. After 1920 the annual rate of net profits was erratic, while during the depression from 1932 until 1935, banks were operating at a loss.

Before 1920 banking profitableness was probably more widely diffused among banks of different size than during subsequent years. Although the number of failures was by no means negligible, the twenty-year period before 1920 was an era of banking prosperity. As noted by a recent writer, "there was a gradual and steady upward swing of the price level, with the result that the collateral held by the banks and the net worth of the unsecured borrower constantly increased in value . . ."[5] In this prosperity all banks joined. But increased competition due to the large increase in the number of banks, a low degree of banking ability among a substantial proportion of the managers of the smaller banks, and the failure to build up adequate reserves had gradually undermined the system, so that when adverse conditions set in, the profitless character of small bank operations became a definite fact, as evidenced by the large number of failures after 1920 and by the record of operations.

Of 7,403 national banks, 4,000 made profits of 6 per cent or more during the five-year period ending June 30, 1930; 1,396 made from 3 up to 6 per cent; 836 made up to 3 per cent; 1,171 had deficits.

---

5. C. D. Bremer, *American Bank Failures*, p. 38.

When these banks are grouped by the size of their loans and investments, it appears that the smaller banks had poorer profit records than the larger. Thirty-five per cent of the smallest class had deficits. The proportion of unprofitable institutions decreased continuously with increasing size.

Forty-six per cent of the 7,403 banks had deficits or profits of less than 6 per cent, but only 20 per cent of the largest banks failed to earn 6 per cent or more. On the other hand, 74 per cent of the smallest banks fell short of this level, which is estimated to be about the minimum necessary to set aside adequate reserves and pay dividends.

Similar relationships between the smaller and the larger banks prevail in each of five geographical regions studied. The study by regions also shows that the smaller institutions made relatively the best showing in the northeastern states and the worst in the western states.

State banks, judged by a sample from Iowa, show an even less favorable distribution of profits than the 7,403 national banks or the national banks in the mid-continent states, of which Iowa forms a part. To illustrate, 42 per cent of the smallest Iowa state banks had deficits, as against 35 per cent and 36 per cent, respectively, of the smallest national banks as a whole and the smallest mid-continent national banks.

This is the situation in regard to profits on invested capital. When, however, the ratio of gross earnings to earning assets or loans and investments is computed, it is found that the smallest banks have generally shown higher ratios than the larger ones, although there is no constant decrease in the rate of gross earnings as banks advance in size. The relationship between the size of earning assets and the several items of expense explains, in general, why, in spite of higher gross earnings, net profits in terms of earning assets are smaller for smaller banks than for larger institutions. Furthermore, because earning assets per hundred dollars of invested capital show a marked tendency to decrease as banks decrease in size, it is to be expected that net profits on invested capital would show a definite increase as banks advance in size.

10. PROFITS OF GROUPS OF LARGE NON-FINANCIAL CORPORATIONS, 1900–1934

The majority of 93 large corporations existing between 1900 and 1903 had, up to 1914, not been profitable for investors in their common stocks, although some were exceptionally profitable.

An analysis of the 1909–1924 period shows that an investment in 200 giant corporations at the beginning of this period would have resulted in a profit in only about 60 per cent of the cases.

The "New Era" between 1919 and 1929 was profitable— but much more profitable for investors than for the corporations in which they invested. If, however, the period from 1919 through 1934 is considered, the investor did not fare so well. If he had bought an equal number of shares in each of 191 large corporations in 1919, his annual appreciation plus his annual cash income would have averaged only 8.4 per cent, instead of 18.9 per cent—the result up to 1929. If he had invested an equal amount in each corporation, his average annual return (cash income plus appreciation) through 1929 would have been 13.9 per cent. But if he had held his securities until 1934, this figure would have been reduced to 3.5 per cent (cash income less depreciation of principal during the depression years).

11. Profits and Dividends of 450 Leading Industrial, Utility and Railroad Corporations, 1927–1935

The Standard Statistics Company tabulation of 450 important corporations shows that the net profit[6] and the net income of industrials and railroads reached their peak in 1929, but that the earnings of the utilities advanced for another year. The utilities, however, did not begin to recover from the depression until 1935, while the earnings of industrials and railroads started to rise in 1933. Railroads suffered most from the depression and utilities least.

Common dividend payments were highest in 1929 for industrials, in 1930 for rails and in 1931 for utilities. For the first two groups they hit a low in 1933; for the last, in 1935. But the low for utility dividends meant a decline of only 16 per cent from 1928, while at their low point industrial dividends were off 58 per cent and rail dividends 78 per cent from that year.

Interesting differences appear when industrial groups are compared. For example, earnings started their decline in textiles in 1928; in tobacco not until 1932. Steel was the most erratic performer of all the industries covered. Its earnings made the biggest gain in 1929 over 1928, but in 1934 steel was

6. Net profit, as used in the Standard Statistics Company tabulation, is the amount available to meet fixed charges.

the only industry to show a deficit instead of a net income. Earnings were most stable in tobacco, chemicals, food and retail trade.

Various industrial groups displayed wide differences also in their dividend records. Common stockholders in steel and iron companies fared worst during the depression, those in tobacco and tobacco products fared best. Those in the chemicals and fertilizer industry, in food products and in retail trade were comparatively fortunate, while those in automobiles and trucks and in electrical equipment and radio suffered severely.

12. Profits and Dividends of 677 Large Corporations, 1928–1934

A study of 677 large corporations—each with assets of at least $1 million—shows that the net income of the group declined 91 per cent between 1928 and 1932, and that total cash dividend payments dropped 35 per cent. When these corporations are divided into four assets classes, the largest class exhibits the smallest income decline, while the second largest exhibits the greatest. Dividends decreased most in the largest class—48 per cent—and least in the second smallest —18 per cent.

There were tremendous variations among the eight main industrial groups.[7] The net income of the two agricultural

7. Since this analysis was based on the reports of the corporations made for publication and not those submitted for tax purposes, there is doubtless less uniformity in accounting practices. Some of the variations reported may, then, be the result of differences in management policies rather than differences in actual operating results.

corporations was 16 per cent lower in 1929 than in 1928, while that of the financial corporations was 46 per cent higher. In 1932, service had a deficit considerably greater than its 1928 net income, while transportation and other public utilities had a net income that was only 29 per cent below 1928. Dividend payments of mining and quarrying corporations were more than seven times as great in 1929 as in 1928, but by 1932 they had fallen to less than half the 1928 figure. On the other hand, the dividends of transportation and other public utilities corporations were 14 per cent higher in 1932 than in 1928, and those of trade firms were only 24 per cent lower in the later year than in the earlier.

When selected groups and sub-groups are compared as to the relationship of the assets classes within each, it becomes clearer than ever that conclusions based on "all industries" data may be misleading when applied to a specific industry. No one assets class makes either the best or the worst showing in all six groups, or even in the majority of them. This is true both of changes in net income and changes in dividends.

Chapter 14

CONCLUSIONS

THE ANALYSIS of *Statistics of Income* has proved conclusively that there are characteristic differences among classes of corporations of various size. Each item that has been studied—gross income, total costs, profits, capital structure, turnover, dividends—supports this conclusion.

To present a composite picture of these differences the following summary table has been prepared. It contains figures for only three size classes: the smallest corporations—those with assets of less than $50,000; the moderately large corporations—those with assets between $1 million and $5 million; and the largest corporations—those with assets of $50 million and over. It covers only the year 1933, or the changes between 1931 and 1933. It is sufficient, however, to establish the existence of size variations.

Is There a Most Profitable Size?

No simple answer to this question can be given. If by profitable, is meant profit on gross income,[1] then it is fair to say that, on the whole, the largest corporations were the most profitable, and that there was a well marked profit trend from the smallest class through the largest, among all corporations and

1. I.e., the ratio of total costs to gross income.

TABLE 36

SUMMARY OF DATA COMPUTED FROM "STATISTICS OF INCOME"

(All Figures Are Percentages)

Items	Table Reference	All Returns			Returns Showing Net Income			Returns Showing No Net Income		
		A	B	C	A	B	C	A	B	C
Changes in gross income, 1931–1933	2	-15.5	-9.2	-22.0	19.4	39.1	11.2	-24.4	-38.2	-41.8
Changes in total costs, 1931–1933	4	-15.9	-10.4	-20.4	20.8	39.6	15.5	-26.1	-36.2	-40.2
Ratio of total costs to gross income, 1933	6	105.5	102.3	97.3	97.4	92.5	90.8	110.3	117.6	106.3
Ratio of net income to net worth, 1933	9	-21.1	-1.9	0.9	8.6	6.7	4.7	-37.8	-7.5	-2.0
Ratio of total profit to total capitalization, 1933	13	-9.6	0.3	2.5	7.0	6.3	4.7	-15.6	-2.8	1.0
Per cent of total capital borrowed, 1933	15	48.1	30.1	34.9	29.9	20.7	29.0	54.6	35.1	38.7
Per cent of total debt floating, 1933	15	78.4	41.9	17.3	86.7	56.5	24.7	76.7	37.2	13.6
Turnover of total capitalization, 1933	16	310.9	53.2	29.5	360.8	92.3	43.4	287.8	32.0	20.5
Changes in dividends, 1931–1933	18	-49.0	-38.2	-50.7	-37.8	-13.6	-22.2	-35.8	-62.1	-74.2
Ratio of dividends to net income, 1933	20	–	–	–	36.0	52.9	102.5	–	–	–
Ratio of net surplus and undivided profits to total capitalization, 1933	22	-51.9	20.6	23.3	4.9	33.0	22.4	-78.1	13.8	23.9
Ratio of total dividends to net worth, 1933	23	2.1	1.8	2.7	3.1	3.6	4.8	1.6	0.7	1.1
Ratio of estimated common dividends to common stock, 1933	23	1.0	1.5	3.6	3.1	5.5	7.0	0.5	-0.5[a]	0.7

LEGEND: A = Assets under $50,000. B = Assets $1 million–$5 million. C = Assets $50 million and over.

a. See footnote c to Table 23.

among money-making corporations. In the money-losing group the giants again made the best showing, but no trend is discernible from class to class. The poorest record was made by the $5 million-to-$10 million class. All classes made fairly close adjustments of costs to changes in gross income during the period covered.

If by profitable is meant, however, the net income on net worth or the total profit on total capitalization, the story changes in a very interesting way. Among money-making corporations the smallest class was the most profitable and the largest the least; and among money-losing corporations the smallest class was the most unprofitable and the largest class the least. There was a fairly regular trend in both groups, somewhat more clearly defined, however, in the unprofitable. When profitable and unprofitable corporations are combined, the trend resembles that for the unprofitable group.[2] The giant class was the only one which, as a whole, showed a net profit in all three years. This fact is, perhaps, sufficient to earn for it the title of "most profitable class."

To summarize, large corporations that made profits made them at lower rates than small ones, while large corporations that lost money lost at lower rates than small ones. Bigness seemed to act as a stabilization factor. It tended to keep rates of profit or loss within a narrow range. Smallness, on the other hand, seemed to be a leverage factor which tended to cause wide swings. The spread of the ratios of net income to net worth in the giant class in 1933 was from an average profit

2. For the reason that in the years covered there were many more unprofitable than profitable corporations.

of 4.7 per cent, reported by those corporations that had net incomes, to an average loss of 2 per cent, reported by corporations without net incomes. This spread was only 6.7 points. In the median class,[3] the range was from a profit of 7.1 per cent to a loss of 8.5 per cent, or 15.6 points. In the smallest class it was from a profit of 8.6 per cent to a loss of 37.8 per cent, or 46.4 points.

The story can be given still a different twist if the variations in officers' compensation and in depreciation and depletion are neutralized by restoring these items of expense to income. When this is done, the larger corporations are in a much less favorable position in relation to the smaller corporations than otherwise.

Banking Profits

A study of banking profits shows clearly that the larger institutions had more favorable operating results than the smaller ones. Thus, the earning reports of an average of 7,403 national banks during 1926–1930 show that either deficits, or profits of less than 6 per cent, were made by 58 per cent of the banks with loans and investments of less than $500,000, and by only 39 per cent of the banks with loans and investments of $500,000 and over. The corresponding percentages for banks with less than $1 million loans and investments and for banks with loans and investments of $1 million and over were 52 and 35, respectively.[4]

3. Total assets of $500,000–$1,000,000.
4. These percentages are based upon the results of operations of 7,403 national banks during 1926–1930.

The comparison between the profitableness of large and small banks leaves little doubt that the advantage is with the former. Nevertheless, the largest banks are by no means always the most profitable. Neither should it be assumed that operation on a smaller scale cannot be made fairly profitable. Many of the smallest institutions must be looked upon, however, as uneconomic units and as constituting weak links in the banking system.

Inverse Relationship Between Size and Turnover

With a few insignificant exceptions, the turnover of total capitalization and of net worth decreases steadily with increasing assets size. In other words, the smaller corporations do more business in relation to their invested capital than the larger ones.

This is important of itself, but it is even more important as an explanation of why the larger corporations show small rates of profits and losses on capital, and why the smaller corporations show large rates. The profit or loss on gross income multiplied by the turnover equals the profit or loss on capital. Therefore, with any given dollar net income or loss, a relatively large turnover—as in the case of the smaller corporations—produces a relatively large rate of profit or loss on capital. A relatively small turnover—as in the case of the larger corporations—produces a relatively small rate.

Larger Corporations Pay More Liberal Dividends

There is a tendency for the ratio of total dividends to net worth, and of common dividends to common stock, to increase as the assets classes increase in size.

Much more significant, however, is the fact that the percentage of net income paid in dividends increases with hardly a break with increasing size of the assets classes.[5] For example, in 1933 the smallest profitable corporations disbursed 36 per cent of their net income in dividends. The median class disbursed 43.5 per cent. The giant corporations distributed not only their entire profit for the year, but also an additional amount taken from the profits of earlier years. These facts have a bearing on any discussion of a tax on undistributed profits of corporations.

Larger Corporations Have Sounder Financial Set-Ups

So far, size relationships have been discussed from the viewpoint of the income statement. There is, however, also the viewpoint of the balance sheet.

On the whole, the larger corporations get a larger proportion of their capital from stockholders, and a smaller proportion from lenders, than do the smaller ones. Borrowed capital must eventually be repaid; stockholders' capital is a permanent investment. Borrowed capital carries interest charges which must be met as part of the cost of doing business; dividends are not costs. For these reasons the larger corporations, with a smaller proportion of borrowed capital in their financial structure, are obviously safer than smaller ones—especially during depressions.

Larger corporations are safer for another reason also. Com-

---

5. In the case of corporations reporting no net income, a steadily increasing negative percentage of the deficit is paid in dividends.

pared with the smaller ones, a larger proportion of their borrowed capital has fixed maturity dates and a smaller proportion is subject to the call of creditors. The trend in this respect
is very sharply defined. In 1933, for example, 78.4 per cent of
the borrowed capital of all corporations in the smallest assets
class was subject to the call of creditors. The percentage
steadily decreased with each larger class until in the giant
class it reached a minimum of 17.3 per cent.

Another balance-sheet factor worth noting is that the larger
corporations have a greater percentage of their total capitalization in the form of surplus and undivided profits than
have the smaller.[6] It is for this reason that the larger corporations were able to pursue more generous dividend policies during the depression than the smaller—they had more to fall
back on.

Size as a Causal Factor

While there is no doubt that there are sharp and significant
differences among classes of corporations of different size, it
is by no means certain that size is the sole cause of these differences. The reason for this doubt is that there are variations
among industrial groups in respect to every factor analyzed.
Since the industrial groups are very unequally represented in
the nine assets classes, what appear to be characteristics of
size may, to some extent at least, be characteristics of industries.

Nevertheless, in general the separate industrial groups

6. In fact, the smallest class (all returns) showed deficits instead of surpluses in 1931, 1932 and 1933, and the second smallest class had deficits in
1932 and 1933. Each of the smallest three classes in the unprofitable group
showed deficits in each of the three years.

show trends that resemble the trends for all industries. There are important exceptions in every case. Here and there an industry displays an almost complete reversal of the all-industry trend. Yet there is a sufficient degree of similarity among industries to justify the conclusion that pure size is one cause— and a very important one—of the differences among the assets classes. There can be no question about the validity of the most important conclusion growing out of the analysis of *Statistics of Income:* Largeness of size has a strong tendency to stabilize the rate of profit on capital. It tends to keep the rate of profit of profitable corporations, and the rate of loss of unprofitable corporations, within comparatively narrow limits.

Studies of Specific Groups of Large Corporations

It is not possible to draw important general conclusions from the studies of specific groups of large corporations. The answer to the question, "how profitable is big business?", depends largely upon what industrial groups are analyzed, which corporations within each group are selected to represent big business, and what period of time is covered. For instance, if the tobacco industry alone were studied during the years between 1929 and 1933, nothing worse than a very mild recession would be detected. If only railroads were analyzed during the years between 1915 and 1920, there would be no indication of the great war and post-war boom.

To draw conclusions from averages is sometimes very deceptive. The majority of 93 large corporations existing between 1900 and 1903 did not prove profitable for their common stockholders during the next fourteen years, but some were very profitable. Only about 60 per cent of 200 giant corporations were profitable investments for those who bought their common stocks in 1919 and sold them in 1924.

It is interesting to note that in some periods stock prices advance more than the earnings of the corporations they represent, while over other periods corporate earnings make a better showing than stock prices. The "New Era" is an example of the former condition; the 1919–1934 period as a whole, an example of the latter.

The Standard Statistics tabulation is interesting for the light it throws on the earnings and dividends of different major industrial groups. The earnings of industrials and railroads reached their peak in 1929, but the earnings of utilities continued to advance for another year. Recovery of rails and industrial earnings started in 1933, while the utilities showed no signs of improvement until 1935. Dividends reached their top in 1929 for industrials, in 1930 for rails and in 1931 for utilities. Their low came in 1933 in the case of the first two groups, but not until 1934 in the case of the last.

Both the Standard Statistics tabulation and the tabulation of the group of 677 corporations prove that dividends are more stable than earnings, and also that dividend changes, as a rule, lag behind changes in earnings, both on the down swing and the up swing.

Millions Affected by Corporate Earnings and Dividends

There are only about half a million corporations in the United States, but these half million businesses are owned by many millions of stockholders. There were only 594 giant corporations in 1933, but several million stockholders were their real owners.

There is no census of the number of stockholders, but estimates have been made. One of the most recent[7] places the number of "book" stockholders at seventeen million in 1927 and twenty-six million in 1932. Eliminating duplication, it is estimated that there were between five and six million different stockholders in 1927 and between ten and twelve million in 1932.

There is general agreement among students that the number of stockholders was at least three times as great in 1928 as in 1900, and that it increased thereafter at least until 1932. Individual corporation reports and income-tax and estate-tax statistics lead to the conclusion that the growth in number of stockholders in recent years has occurred mainly in three periods. From 1916 to 1923 there was a great increase, apparently consisting mainly of persons with incomes under $5,000. After a brief reaction in 1924–1926 the second period began, with an increase in the number of individual stockholders, both wealthy individuals and those in more moderate circumstances. There was an especially large increase in the amount of stock owned by other corporations. The third period began with the crash of 1929 and was characterized by a redistribution of existing stocks among a larger number of owners. The number of stockholders increased greatly until 1932, but whether the proportion owned by wealthy holders increased or decreased cannot be ascertained as yet. Moreover nothing

7. Twentieth Century Fund, Inc., *The Security Markets,* pp. 50–53.

conclusive is known as to developments in 1932 and subsequently.

A large proportion of stockholders is represented by the comparatively small group of larger corporations—the twenty-odd thousand that had assets of $1 million or over in 1933. It is these corporations whose securities are most widely owned.[8] It is they whose securities are listed on the exchanges where they can be purchased by any one with the necessary cash or credit. The smaller corporations, on the other hand, and especially the vast group of the smallest, are undoubtedly to a very large extent owned by a handful of stockholders each.

Furthermore, there were, it has been estimated,[9] between six and ten million individual owners of corporate bonds at the end of 1932, and all these bondholders are as vitally concerned as stockholders in the welfare of the corporations in which their savings are invested. And beyond that, of course, there are many millions of other individuals who have an indirect, but none the less real, stake in the prosperity of corporations—especially the largest—because of investment in corporate securities on the part of insurance companies, banks, public institutions of many kinds, and, today, even of the Federal Government itself.

It is well to bear these facts in mind when assessing the import of data brought out in this and the preceding volume of this series.

8. Of course there are exceptions. The Ford Motor Car Company, for example, is a privately owned giant corporation.

9. Twentieth Century Fund, Inc., *op. cit.*, p. 48.

APPENDICES

Appendix A

CONCLUSIONS OF OTHER STUDIES

Summers' Study of 1,130 Corporations[1]

H. B. Summers studied the reports of 1,130 American and Canadian companies from 1910 to 1929, inclusive, to learn the ratio of net income to total permanent investment. He compared the total of interest on bonds and dividends on stocks plus the annual increases in surplus, with the sum of capital stock, funded debt and surplus.

The companies were classified in nine industrial groups and in seven size classes within each group. The smallest class comprised corporations with invested capital of less than $2 million; the largest, with invested capital of more than $100 million.

For all industrial groups combined, the highest average earnings were in the smallest class; and this was true also of five of the nine industrial groups. In machinery and in textiles the $5 million-to-$10 million class was the most profitable. In hardware and in food-stuffs the $25 million-to-$50 million class was in the lead. In no group was the highest class the most profitable. Hardware was the only exception

1. H. B. Summers, "A Comparison of the Rates of Earning of Large-Scale and Small-Scale Industries," *The Quarterly Journal of Economics,* May 1932, pp. 465–479.

to the tendency of earning rates to decrease with increasing investment. Summers concluded that ". . . with certain exceptions, heavy investment is apparently a disadvantage, rather than an advantage, in securing high rates of earnings."[2]

Studies by Crum and Bowman Confirm Summers' Conclusion[3]

Crum has shown by an analysis of 1926 income statistics that the ratio of net income to total assets increased with the size of the net income up to about $100,000, but, except for construction and agriculture, not significantly thereafter.[4] It is impossible to say what amount of capital is typical of that size income.

Another study by Crum,[5] covering the depression year 1931, brings out the fact that of those corporations showing a profit, the highest ratios of net income to net worth[6] were in the class that had assets of less than $50,000 each. This was true of six of the seven major groups analyzed by Crum, the exception being trade where the $50 million-and-over class showed the highest profit ratio. It was true also of four of the sub-groups of manufacturing that were studied. Here the exception was the chemical industry in which the highest profit ratio was earned by the $5 million-to-$10 million assets class.

If, however, the profitable and unprofitable corporations

2. *Ibid.*, p. 479.

3. William Leonard Crum, *Corporate Earning Power;* Raymond T. Bowman, *A Statistical Study of Profits.*

4. Crum, *op. cit.*, pp. 310–311.

5. *The Effect of Size on Corporate Earnings and Condition.* See especially pp. 15–16.

6. Capital stock, surplus and undivided profits—less deficits—is known as net worth.

are considered together, the smallest assets class showed a loss in each industrial group. For the entire manufacturing division and for trade, the only assets class to show a net income was that composed of corporations each owning assets of $50 million and over. In the public utilities division, net incomes were reported for all corporations with assets of $250,000 and over, the most profitable corporations being in the $250,000-to-$500,000 class. Corporations with assets of $50 million and over were also the only ones to show a net income in two of the manufacturing sub-groups—metals and foods.

Bowman has concluded that for the years 1914 to 1925 "the highest size-group very seldom makes the highest earning rate" and that "on the whole, the higher earning rates seem to be associated more closely with small size than with large size, although this generalization does not hold true for all industries, or for the same industry in different years." The safest generalization that can be drawn, Bowman states, is that "size and earnings ratios are not correlated highly, either positively or negatively. . . ."[7]

Epstein's Analysis of Corporate Reports[8]

Epstein has analyzed the income-tax reports of 2,046 manufacturing corporations from 1919 to 1928, especially those for 1924 and 1928. In 1928 less than 2 per cent of these corporations had capital of under $250,000; less than 28 per cent had under $1 million. At the other extreme were 82 corporations

7. *Op. cit.,* p. 114. Cf. also pp. 102–122. Bowman's analysis, summarized above, is based on his study of eight businesses (seven manufacturing and one retail) for various years from 1914 to 1925, inclusive.
8. Ralph C. Epstein, *Industrial Profits in the United States.*

—about 4 per cent of the total number—each with capital of $50 million or over.[9]

As a group, these 2,046 manufacturing corporations earned at a higher rate than the more than 300,000 other corporations making income-tax returns. The most profitable class, however, was that composed of corporations with a capital of less than $500,000, and averaging $350,000. This was true whether the test was the ratio of net income to net worth or the ratio of total profit to total capitalization.

"Beyond question," comments Epstein, "among manufacturing corporations of all sizes of capital from $250,000 to over $50,000,000, the smaller corporations earn profits at higher rates than the larger ones."[10] The class with capital of less than $500,000 showed a rate of return of more than 20 per cent; the class with capital of $50 million and over, of less than 10 per cent. The advantage of the smaller companies was especially great in the food and in the chemical industries.[11]

Epstein demonstrated also[12] that from 1924 to 1928 a group of 3,144 corporations, including the 2,046 manufacturing corporations—less than 2 per cent of which had a capital of under $250,000—earned at a higher rate than the more than 300,000 other corporations which filed tax returns, but at a lower rate than some 200,000 corporations that had net incomes. In other words, if small corporations made any money at all they tended to earn higher rates of net income on their stock capitalization, and higher rates of profit on their total

9. *Ibid.*, pp. 50–57, 131–138.
10. *Ibid.*, p. 132.
11. *Ibid.*, pp. 133–137.
12. *Ibid.*, pp. 50, 53, 58.

capitalization, than large corporations. The four industries found by Epstein to have been the most consistently profitable —scientific instruments, toilet preparations, miscellaneous printing and publishing, and retail automobiles—comprised small corporations. The one that was most consistently among the least profitable was meat packing, in which the average capital per concern was more than $50 million.

Paton's Analysis[13]

W. A. Paton has analyzed for the years 1927–1929 the audit reports of 714 small and medium-size corporations,[14] predominantly in manufacturing and trade, and has measured their profitability from two standards—average rate of earnings on net assets and average rate on stockholders' equity. Paton's figures indicate that for the 714 companies as a whole, as well as for manufacturing concerns as a group, corporations with assets between $50,000 and $200,000 earned on the average at a higher rate on their assets than either smaller or larger ones. In trading, however, the most profitable concerns fell in the two classes, $500,000–$1,500,000, and over $5 million. No consistent differences in earnings between large and small concerns were evidenced within the sub-groups of the industrial branches covered.[15]

Measured in terms of their average rate of earnings on

13. W. A. Paton, *Corporate Profits as Shown by Audit Reports.*
14. The average size of these corporations in terms of net book assets (total book assets less accrued depreciation and other valuation reserves) ranged from $306,692 for the construction industry to $3,450,385 for the extraction group. No very large corporations are included in this study.
15. Paton, *op. cit.*, pp. 4–5, 73–76.

stockholders' equity, the figures for all corporations indicated a slightly higher rate of profit for larger companies. For manufacturing, however, the smaller concerns tended to show the more favorable earnings.[16]

Taking the industrial groups separately, the ratio of earnings to both net book value of assets and to stockholders' equity was higher for the larger companies in construction, trading, real estate and finance, and service, but higher for the smaller companies in the extraction group and in manufacturing.[17] Further classification into 54 sub-groups showed that, when the ratio of earnings to net book value of assets was considered, the larger companies were more profitable in 28 industries, and the smaller ones in 26. Among the sub-groups in which larger companies had the most decided advantage were shoes; wholesale and retail auto supplies, electrical equipment, radios, sporting goods; advertising; printing, publishing, lithographing, etc. The sub-groups in which the smaller companies had the most decided advantage were oil and gas extraction; cotton and wool merchants; fruit, vegetables, dairy products, grain, etc.; laundering and dry cleaning.[18]

Results of National Industrial Conference Board's Study[19]

A study of more than four thousand trading and manufacturing corporations covering the years 1918–1925 was made

16. *Ibid.*, p. 57.
17. *Ibid.*, pp. 20–21, 42–43.
18. *Ibid.*, pp. 21–34.
19. *Shifting and Effects of Federal Corporation Income Tax*, I, 36–42, 222–224.

by the National Industrial Conference Board, Inc. All of these were corporations that survived from 1918 to 1925 and had net incomes of $100,000 or more in at least one of those years. Their capital ranged from $100,000 to more than $1 million. The analysis showed that the most profitable group in each year—the group that made more than 20 per cent on its capital—had a smaller average capital than the average of all corporations studied.

The Two Hundred Largest Corporations of Berle and Means[20]

One method of testing the efficiency of large corporations is to study their rate of growth and compare it with the growth of other corporations. Berle and Means have made a very extensive study of this nature. The authors conclude, as is shown by the quotation that follows, that the concentration of assets in the possession of the 200 largest non-financial corporations was at a much more rapid rate than the increase of corporate assets as a whole.

When the rates of growth of the wealth of all non-financial corporations and of the assets of the 200 largest corporations are thus compared, they show the large corporations as a group to be growing very much more rapidly than all corporations. For the period from 1909 to 1928 their annual rate of growth has been 5.4 per cent, while that of all corporations (assuming the estimates are reliable) has amounted to only 3.6 per cent, and for corporations other than the largest 200 only 2.0 per cent. The large corporations would thus appear to be increasing in wealth over 50 per cent faster than all corporations or over two and one-half times as fast as smaller corpora-

20. A. A. Berle, Jr. and Gardiner C. Means, *The Modern Corporation and Private Property.*

tions. From 1921 to 1928 the annual rate of growth of the large corporations has been 6.1 per cent compared with 4.4 per cent for all corporations or 3.1 per cent for the smaller companies. From 1924 to 1928, a period of most rapid growth, the annual rates were respectively 7.7 per cent for the large, 4.9 per cent for all, and only 2.6 per cent for corporations other than the largest 200, indicating that the large corporations were growing more than half again as fast as all corporations and three times as fast as smaller corporations.

This very much more rapid rate of growth of the big companies in comparison to other companies is equally evident when we examine the proportion of the income of all non-banking corporations which has been reported each year by the 200 companies reporting the largest incomes.[21]

It should be pointed out that some students question the validity of these conclusions because of the statistical methods that were used by Berle and Means.[22] They also call attention to the fact that the 200 largest non-financial corporations are not the same from year to year, and that the roster has changed greatly since 1909, only 83 of the 200 giants of 1909 still remaining on the list in 1934.

21. *Ibid.,* pp. 35, 37.
22. See, for example, Rufus S. Tucker, "Increasing Concentration of Business Not Supported by Statistical Evidence," *The Annalist,* July 31, 1936, pp. 149–150; also W. L. Crum, "On the Alleged Concentration of Economic Power," *The American Economic Review,* March 1934, pp. 69–83. The same issue of *The American Economic Review* contains "A Reply by Gardiner C. Means" on pp. 84–87, and "A Rejoinder by W. L. Crum" on pp. 87–88.

Appendix B

TABLE 37

NUMERICAL DATA FOR TABLE 9a

(All Figures in Thousands of Dollars)

Total Assets Classes	Year	All Returns		Returns Showing Net Income		Returns Showing No Net Income	
		Net Worth	Net Income[b]	Net Worth	Net Income	Net Worth	Net Income[b]
Under 50	1931	1,909,806	− 415,247	909,192	105,294	1,000,614	− 520,540
	1932	1,857,591	− 613,435	452,485	39,460	1,405,107	− 652,895
	1933	1,825,483	− 385,923	655,634	56,185	1,169,848	− 442,108
50–100	1931	2,403,734	− 218,309	1,087,025	85,712	1,316,708	− 304,021
	1932	2,266,602	− 316,959	566,624	35,712	1,699,979	− 352,671
	1933	2,151,998	− 121,794	802,770	55,707	1,349,229	− 177,501
100–250	1931	5,393,995	− 352,921	2,379,901	166,508	3,014,094	− 519,429
	1932	4,997,878	− 494,531	1,294,585	78,488	3,703,293	− 573,019
	1933	4,722,099	− 208,808	1,833,995	127,070	2,888,103	− 335,878
250–500	1931	5,756,104	− 267,548	2,461,529	168,201	3,294,573	− 435,749
	1932	5,311,368	− 390,540	1,468,639	88,777	3,842,728	− 479,316
	1933	4,934,775	− 151,410	1,990,024	141,479	2,964,751	− 292,890
500–1,000	1931	7,032,788	− 271,664	2,837,485	186,790	4,195,302	− 458,454
	1932	6,447,920	− 409,125	1,807,385	106,957	4,640,535	− 516,082
	1933	6,086,910	− 128,467	2,495,318	176,876	3,591,593	− 305,343

TABLE 37 (Continued)

Total Assets Classes	Year	All Returns		Returns Showing Net Income		Returns Showing No Net Income	
		Net Worth	Net Income[b]	Net Worth	Net Income	Net Worth	Net Income[b]
1,000–5,000	1931	19,742,973	− 591,129	7,533,326	487,702	12,209,649	−1,078,831
	1932	18,302,785	− 869,195	5,023,323	279,483	13,279,462	−1,148,678
	1933	17,204,857	− 325,565	6,803,592	456,501	10,401,265	−− 782,066
5,000–10,000	1931	9,275,379	− 166,124	3,679,518	258,963	5,595,862	− 425,087
	1932	8,887,501	− 356,054	2,846,491	167,515	6,041,010	− 523,568
	1933	8,468,995	− 143,036	3,593,368	232,818	4,875,626	− 375,854
10,000–50,000	1931	22,044,544	− 104,011	9,668,497	672,317	12,376,046	− 776,328
	1932	20,372,962	− 542,778	6,656,872	392,370	13,716,090	− 935,149
	1933	19,711,597	− 145,979	8,894,999	597,600	10,816,597	− 743,579
50,000 and over	1931	69,703,566	1,506,995	30,106,973	2,117,862	39,596,593	− 610,868
	1932	65,123,912	199,828	22,889,555	1,225,917	42,234,357	−1,026,089
	1933	62,451,298	555,335	27,025,397	1,258,199	35,425,902	− 702,864
All corporations	1931	143,262,890	− 879,958	60,663,447	4,249,349	82,599,444	−5,129,307
	1932	133,568,517	−3,792,789	43,005,956	2,414,679	90,562,560	−6,207,467
	1933	127,578,013	−1,055,647	54,095,096	3,102,435	73,482,915	−4,158,082

a. *Statistics of Income*, page references same as for Table 2.
b. Minus signs indicate deficits.

Appendix C

TABLE 38

Numerical Data for Table 13[a]

(All Figures in Thousands of Dollars)

Total Assets Classes	Year	All Returns		Returns Showing Net Income		Returns Showing No Net Income	
		Total Capitalization	Total Profit[b]	Total Capitalization	Total Profit	Total Capitalization	Total Profit[b]
Under 50	1931	3,441,195	−359,622	1,316,065	120,749	2,125,130	− 480,370
	1932	3,520,081	−558,518	639,601	46,209	2,880,482	− 604,728
	1933	3,514,176	−335,589	935,070	65,729	2,579,103	− 401,317
50–100	1931	4,050,931	−151,788	1,602,174	107,755	2,448,757	− 259,543
	1932	3,876,205	−256,389	776,081	44,649	3,100,124	− 301,038
	1933	3,631,067	− 67,634	1,110,090	67,525	2,520,978	− 135,159
100–250	1931	8,813,834	−189,362	3,526,850	225,529	5,286,984	− 414,891
	1932	8,204,551	−349,495	1,774,858	102,539	6,429,693	− 452,033
	1933	7,817,954	− 82,949	2,489,574	154,633	5,328,379	− 237,582
250–500	1931	9,050,530	− 88,853	3,506,946	230,170	5,543,581	− 319,022
	1932	8,297,456	−239,779	1,946,646	113,566	6,350,809	− 353,344
	1933	7,792,866	− 22,038	2,607,093	168,182	5,185,773	− 190,221
500–1,000	1931	10,592,606	− 58,101	3,901,015	253,865	6,691,590	− 311,966
	1932	9,676,781	−227,874	2,351,339	136,854	7,325,441	− 364,729
	1933	9,160,056	23,434	3,166,426	207,449	5,993,631	− 184,015

TABLE 38 (Continued)

Total Assets Classes	Year	All Returns		Returns Showing Net Income		Returns Showing No Net Income	
		Total Capitalization	Total Profit[b]	Total Capitalization	Total Profit	Total Capitalization	Total Profit[b]
1,000–5,000	1931	28,101,872	– 23,455	9,873,795	658,837	18,228,079	– 682,291
	1932	25,952,670	–382,508	6,495,583	361,709	19,457,088	– 744,218
	1933	24,598,623	82,498	8,574,774	536,218	16,023,849	– 453,720
5,000–10,000	1931	13,099,730	97,039	4,736,310	335,629	8,363,421	– 238,591
	1932	12,663,479	–124,874	3,640,253	208,556	9,023,226	– 333,429
	1933	12,114,823	54,014	4,500,343	270,502	7,614,480	– 216,488
10,000–50,000	1931	31,306,391	497,513	12,796,769	874,668	18,509,622	– 377,156
	1932	29,129,290	– 29,880	9,084,977	509,517	20,044,313	– 539,398
	1933	28,297,027	297,293	11,628,052	717,289	16,668,974	– 419,996
50,000 and over	1931	106,158,158	3,765,598	43,603,273	2,910,207	62,554,884	855,391
	1932	100,120,693	2,282,807	32,106,654	1,743,245	68,014,039	539,562
	1933	95,895,465	2,370,660	38,060,085	1,787,923	57,835,381	582,738
All corporations	1931	214,615,247	3,488,969	84,863,199	5,717,408	129,752,051	–2,228,439
	1932	201,441,203	113,490	58,815,989	3,266,844	142,625,214	–3,153,352
	1933	192,822,057	2,319,690	73,071,507	3,975,450	119,750,548	–1,655,760

a. *Statistics of Income*, page references same as for Table 2.
b. Minus signs indicate deficits.

Appendix D

ADJUSTED RATIO OF NET INCOME TO NET WORTH

THE RELATIVE profitableness of corporations of different sizes is perhaps not precisely measured by the ratio of net income to net worth. There is a lack of uniformity in accounting methods and practices and in financial policies, with the result that net income is unlikely to mean exactly the same thing for any two corporations.

It is, of course, impossible to make the data in *Statistics of Income* entirely consistent as among assets classes or industrial groups, and thus it is impossible to measure relative profitableness with entire accuracy. But two of the important factors that create inconsistency can be eliminated—compensation of officers and depreciation and depletion.[1]

Depreciation and Depletion Practices of Small and Large Corporations

Table 39 shows the differences in depreciation and depletion rates among corporations in the various assets classes.

With a few exceptions depreciation and depletion rates decrease with the increasing size of corporations. Several factors

1. See footnote 2, pp. 41–42.

TABLE 39

DEPRECIATION PLUS DEPLETION AS PERCENTAGES OF CAPITAL ASSETS, BY
TOTAL ASSETS CLASSES, 1931, 1932 AND 1933[a]

(*Total Assets Classes in Thousands of Dollars*)

Total Assets Classes	Percentages								
	All Corporations			Corporations Reporting Net Income			Corporations Reporting No Net Income		
	1931	1932	1933	1931	1932	1933	1931	1932	1933
Under 50	9.4	9.3	8.9	8.0	8.9	10.4	10.3	9.4	8.6
50–100	6.6	5.9	5.7	7.1	6.9	8.0	6.3	5.6	5.0
100–250	5.0	4.7	4.7	5.4	6.0	7.0	4.7	4.4	4.0
250–500	4.3	4.2	4.1	4.9	5.5	6.2	3.9	3.8	3.4
500–1,000	4.1	3.9	4.0	4.7	5.0	5.9	3.8	3.6	3.3
1,000–5,000	3.9	3.9	4.0	4.2	4.3	5.3	3.8	3.8	3.4
5,000–10,000	3.8	3.7	3.9	4.0	4.1	4.8	3.6	3.6	3.4
10,000–50,000	4.1	4.0	4.1	4.3	4.0	4.6	4.0	4.0	3.7
50,000 and over	3.1	3.0	2.9	3.4	3.5	3.8	2.8	2.7	2.3
All corporations	3.6	3.6	3.5	3.9	3.9	4.5	3.4	3.4	3.0

a. Computed from data in *Statistics of Income,* page references same as for Table 2.
Capital assets represent lands, buildings and equipment (less depreciation).

may account for this. For example, the Treasury may examine
the depreciation charges of the larger corporations more care-
fully than those of the smaller. Better maintenance by the
larger corporations may permit lower annual depreciation
rates than could safely be charged by the smaller corporations.
The composition of the capital assets of larger corporations is
likely to differ from that of the smaller ones. The proportion
of the smaller corporations that rent the premises they occupy
is, presumably, larger than the proportion of the larger ones.
If that is true, then the smaller corporations have a greater

percentage of their capital assets in equipment than the larger corporations, and equipment depreciates at a much higher annual rate than lands or buildings.

Whatever the explanation, there is a remarkably smooth trend of lessening depreciation and depletion rates with increasing assets size. In five out of nine instances, however, the rates of the $1 million-to-$5 million class were as high as, or higher than, those of the $500,000-to-$1,000,000; and in seven out of nine, the rates of the $10 million-to-$50 million class were higher than those of the immediately smaller one.

Table 40 shows the effects of restoring to net income the cost of compensation of officers and of depreciation and depletion.

The ratios in Table 40 do not represent actual profits, either for income-tax purposes or from the point of view of stockholders, but for convenience they will be referred to as adjusted profit ratios. Their significance is as measures of what the relative profitableness of corporations of different sizes would be if compensation to officers had the same weight in the income statement of corporations of every size class, and if depreciation and depletion were charged at the same percentage of capital assets by all corporations. It may be that the adjusted ratios measure the profitableness of corporations better than the more conventional standards.

If these conditions were facts, it becomes clear by comparing Tables 9 and 40 that the larger corporations would occupy a much less favorable position in relation to the smaller ones than they do when net income is left unadjusted. Only the high points of the comparison can be brought out.

TABLE 40

RATIO OF NET INCOME PLUS COMPENSATION OF OFFICERS PLUS DEPRECIATION AND DEPLETION, TO NET WORTH, BY ASSETS CLASSES, 1931, 1932 AND 1933[a]

(Money Figures and Total Assets Classes in Thousands of Dollars; Ratios in Percentages)

Total Assets Classes	Year	All Returns			Returns Showing Net Income			Returns Showing No Net Income		
		Net Worth (A)	Net Income Plus Compensation of Officers Plus Depreciation and Depletion[b] (B)	Ratio (B/A)	Net Worth (A)	Net Income Plus Compensation of Officers Plus Depreciation and Depletion (B)	Ratio (B/A)	Net Worth (A)	Net Income Plus Compensation of Officers Plus Depreciation and Depletion[b] (B)	Ratio (B/A)
Under 50	1931	1,909,806	235,676	12.3	909,192	340,391	37.4	1,000,614	−104,712	−10.5
	1932	1,857,591	7,092	0.4	452,485	150,396	33.2	1,405,107	−143,304	−10.2
	1933	1,825,483	228,126	12.5	655,634	243,180	37.1	1,169,848	−15,055	−1.3
50–100	1931	2,403,734	214,887	8.9	1,087,025	272,350	25.1	1,316,708	−57,464	−4.4
	1932	2,266,602	32,624	1.4	566,624	120,230	21.2	1,699,979	−87,605	−5.2
	1933	2,151,998	203,217	9.4	802,770	189,802	23.6	1,349,229	13,415	1.0
100–250	1931	5,393,995	296,689	5.5	2,379,901	454,053	19.1	3,014,094	−157,364	−5.2
	1932	4,997,878	34,174	0.7	1,294,585	220,206	17.0	3,703,293	−186,032	−5.0
	1933	4,722,099	281,350	6.0	1,833,995	344,166	18.8	2,888,103	−62,815	−2.2
250–500	1931	5,756,104	224,209	3.9	2,461,529	387,526	15.7	3,294,573	−163,317	−5.0
	1932	5,311,368	10,306	0.2	1,468,639	207,586	14.1	3,842,728	−197,277	−5.1
	1933	4,954,775	215,295	4.4	1,990,024	310,228	15.6	2,964,751	−94,934	−3.2
500–1,000	1931	7,052,788	182,166	2.6	2,837,485	379,648	13.4	4,195,302	−197,482	−4.7
	1932	6,447,920	−33,531	−0.5	1,807,385	219,437	12.1	4,640,535	−252,968	−5.5
	1933	6,086,910	221,221	3.6	2,495,318	337,639	13.5	3,591,593	−116,418	−3.2

TABLE 40 (Continued)

Total Assets Classes	Year	All Returns			Returns Showing Net Income			Returns Showing No Net Income		
		Net Worth (A)	Net Income Plus Compensation of Officers Plus Depreciation and Depletionb (B)	Ratio (B/A)	Net Worth (A)	Net Income Plus Compensation of Officers Plus Depreciation and Depletion (B)	Ratio (B/A)	Net Worth (A)	Net Income Plus Compensation of Officers Plus Depreciation and Depletionb (B)	Ratio (B/A)
1,000–5,000	1931	19,742,973	289,950	1.5	7,533,326	831,876	11.0	12,209,649	− 541,926	− 4.4
	1932	18,302,785	− 97,943	−0.5	5,023,323	488,578	9.7	13,279,462	− 586,521	− 4.4
	1933	17,204,857	393,068	2.3	6,803,592	766,350	11.3	10,401,265	− 373,282	− 3.6
5,000–10,000	1931	9,275,379	167,428	1.8	3,679,518	390,411	10.6	5,595,862	− 222,982	− 4.0
	1932	8,887,501	− 44,315	−0.5	2,846,491	266,315	9.4	6,041,010	− 310,629	− 5.1
	1933	8,468,995	156,861	1.9	3,593,368	367,111	10.2	4,875,626	− 210,250	− 4.3
10,000–50,000	1931	22,044,544	664,911	3.0	9,668,497	1,012,512	10.5	12,376,046	− 347,599	− 2.8
	1932	20,372,962	146,920	0.7	6,656,872	615,058	9.2	13,716,090	− 468,138	− 3.4
	1933	19,711,597	522,105	2.7	8,894,999	899,185	10.1	10,816,597	− 377,080	− 3.5
50,000 and over	1931	69,703,566	3,611,301	5.2	30,106,973	3,084,360	10.2	39,596,593	526,941	1.3
	1932	65,123,912	2,081,601	3.2	22,889,555	1,957,883	8.6	42,234,357	123,718	0.3
	1933	62,451,298	2,317,228	3.7	27,025,397	2,103,296	7.8	35,425,902	213,932	0.6
All corporations	1931	143,262,890	5,887,215	4.1	60,663,447	7,153,124	11.8	82,599,444	−1,265,907	− 1.5
	1932	133,568,517	2,136,930	1.6	43,005,956	4,245,687	9.9	90,562,560	−2,108,756	− 2.3
	1933	127,578,013	4,538,468	3.6	54,095,096	5,560,957	10.3	73,482,915	−1,022,489	− 1.4

a. Computed from data in *Statistics of Income*, page references same as for Table 2.   b. Minus signs indicate deficits.

All Corporations

When all returns are considered, the best showing is no longer made by the largest corporations, except in 1932. In that year there is no apparent correlation between size and the adjusted profit ratio. In 1931 and 1933, not the largest but the smallest corporations make the best showing. In 1931 the ratios decrease as size decreases through the $1 million-to-$5 million assets class, after which they rise. In 1932, the $5 million-to-$10 million class marks the bottom of the downward trend.

Profitable and Unprofitable Corporations Separately

For profitable corporations, the adjusted ratios show the same general trend as the unadjusted—decreasing profitableness with increasing size in each of the three years.[2] But the range is much greater in the adjusted ratio series than in the unadjusted, with the adjustment improving the status of the smaller corporations in relation to the larger.

For unprofitable corporations, the general contours of the adjusted ratio trends are similar to those of the unadjusted in 1931 and 1932, although they have more breaks. In both these years, for both series of ratios, the poorest results were achieved by the smallest corporations and the best by the largest. For some reason, however, the adjusted ratio trend becomes very irregular in 1933. In that year the worst showing was made by the $5 million-to-$10 million assets class. The $50,000-to-$100,000 class was in first position, but its lead

2. In the case of the unadjusted series there are breaks in the trend each year; in the case of the adjusted, there are no breaks in any year.

over the $50 million-and-over class was so small as to be insignificant. In the unadjusted ratio series, it will be remembered, the $50,000-to-$100,000 corporations showed losses larger than any other class except the very smallest.

Variations Among Industries

As always, industrial groups and sub-groups show important deviations from the trend. This can be seen in the following three tables which are presented without analysis.

TABLE 41

RATIO OF NET INCOME PLUS COMPENSATION OF OFFICERS PLUS DEPRECIATION AND DEPLETION, TO NET WORTH, BY INDUSTRIAL GROUPS AND BY ASSETS CLASSES, 1932: ALL CORPORATIONS[a]

(Total Assets Classes in Thousands of Dollars; Ratios in Percentages)

Industrial Groups	Total	Under 50	50–100	100–250	250–500	500–1,000	1,000–5,000	5,000–10,000	10,000–50,000	Over 50,000	Classes Grouped[b]
Mining	1.5	− 12.8	2.6	4.4	4.6	2.1	2.3	1.8	2.3	0.2	—
Total manufacturing	1.9	4.1	2.9	1.6	0.6	0.4	c	0.7	0.1	3.6	—
Food	6.3	11.5	10.2	7.5	7.2	6.8	5.0	0.4	2.8	9.0	—
Tobacco	14.9	6.5	3.5	8.9	5.9	c	5.0	b	b	17.2	9.9
Textiles	− 0.7	1.8	1.3	1.1	0.7	− 0.7	− 0.3	− 3.4	b	b	1.1
Leather	− 0.7	− 6.0	1.3	2.9	− 4.5	− 4.8	− 3.0	− 4.9	b	b	4.5
Rubber	1.1	11.6	10.6	1.2	4.2	− 1.9	4.5	—	b	b	1.4
Forest products	− 5.0	− 21.5	− 11.4	− 8.4	− 9.9	− 6.3	b	b	− 4.3	− 1.3	− 3.6
Paper	1.9	9.1	10.3	7.7	5.6	5.7	2.3	4.2	b	b	0.4
Printing	6.2	20.4	10.7	10.1	9.5	7.3	5.8	9.1	b	b	2.8
Chemicals	5.8	5.4	7.3	6.6	6.9	7.1	8.4	7.9	4.9	5.6	—
Stone	0.3	− 8.2	− 1.2	− 1.1	− 2.6	− 1.0	− 1.0	− 1.1	b	b	2.3
Metal	− 1.8	− 5.6	− 1.1	− 2.8	− 3.1	− 2.7	− 4.3	− 2.2	− 3.4	− 0.4	—
Construction	4.8	4.7	5.7	4.7	4.2	2.8	5.1	b	b	b	5.7
Transportation and other public utilities	3.8	22.7	13.6	10.9	6.7	1.3	4.9	3.4	5.3	3.6	—
Trade	1.3	1.8	1.5	0.1	− 0.6	− 0.4	− 0.7	1.5	2.3	6.0	—
Service	− 3.6	9.5	− 3.6	2.2	− 0.3	− 1.5	− 4.4	− 5.5	b	b	− 6.6
Finance	− 1.1	− 17.5	− 2.1	− 2.5	− 1.8	− 2.6	− 2.4	− 4.0	− 1.4	2.2	—
All corporations	1.6	0.4	1.4	0.7	0.2	0.5	0.5	0.5	0.7	3.2	—

a. Based in part on special tabulations made by the Bureau of Internal Revenue for the Twentieth Century Fund for 1932 only. Minus signs indicate deficits.

b. Classes grouped by Bureau of Internal Revenue to conceal data reported and identity of corporations.

c. Less than one-tenth of 1 per cent.

TABLE 42

RATIO OF NET INCOME PLUS COMPENSATION OF OFFICERS PLUS DEPRECIATION AND DEPLETION, TO NET WORTH, BY INDUSTRIAL GROUPS AND BY ASSETS CLASSES, 1932: PROFITABLE CORPORATIONS[a]

(Total Assets Classes in Thousands of Dollars; Ratios in Percentages)

Industrial Groups	Total	Total Assets Classes									
		Under 50	50–100	100–250	250–500	500–1,000	1,000–5,000	5,000–10,000	10,000–50,000	Over 50,000	Classes Grouped[b]
Mining	7.4	45.1	20.4	16.2	13.6	10.6	7.4	5.8	6.2	4.7	—
Total manufacturing	10.7	40.9	27.9	21.8	17.5	13.1	12.2	11.9	10.0	8.4	—
Food	12.0	35.5	27.2	21.8	18.2	17.7	12.1	11.1	10.9	10.4	—
Tobacco	16.5	47.5	16.1	19.8	15.4	8.7	11.7	13.3	14.5	17.2	—
Textiles	23.7	47.6	33.0	23.1	18.7	12.8	10.4	7.9	b	b	7.4
Leather	11.5	45.3	31.9	25.1	17.4	13.4	13.8	11.1	b	b	8.0
Rubber	6.8	49.4	35.3	26.8	14.1	17.8	9.8	–	–	b	9.2
Forest products	11.9	27.0	23.0	16.1	11.6	8.8	b	b	–	–	10.2
Paper	10.9	49.6	30.1	23.5	17.4	14.3	11.6	10.5	b	b	6.2
Printing	9.6	46.7	26.8	22.7	18.1	17.4	12.9	13.9	b	b	4.3
Chemicals	14.9	41.1	27.1	23.4	19.6	18.2	15.9	15.7	9.9	7.0	—
Stone	9.5	24.0	22.2	20.9	19.0	12.4	10.1	9.1	b	b	7.3
Metal	10.4	40.3	27.6	18.9	15.7	12.7	10.4	10.0	11.5	7.0	—
Construction	23.8	56.9	41.4	32.2	27.0	16.5	18.7	b	b	–	19.0
Transportation and other public utilities	8.4	31.0	24.3	18.9	15.2	13.6	10.2	8.2	9.3	7.9	—
Trade	14.0	31.9	21.6	18.2	15.7	14.1	11.2	10.4	12.4	11.4	—
Service	2.6	29.6	13.5	7.4	3.2	3.1	0.5	– 1.0	b	b	– 3.5
Finance	8.1	18.4	11.2	9.6	7.9	7.0	6.0	6.2	6.8	11.3	—
All corporations	9.9	33.2	21.2	17.0	14.1	12.1	9.7	9.4	9.2	8.6	—

a. Same as footnote a, Table 41.   b. Same as footnote b, Table 41.

TABLE 43

RATIO OF NET INCOME PLUS COMPENSATION OF OFFICERS PLUS DEPRECIATION AND DEPLETION, TO NET WORTH, BY INDUSTRIAL GROUPS AND BY ASSETS CLASSES, 1932: UNPROFITABLE CORPORATIONS[a]

(Total Assets Classes in Thousands of Dollars; Ratios in Percentages)

Industrial Groups	Total Assets Classes										
	Total	Under 50	50–100	100–250	250–500	500–1,000	1,000–5,000	5,000–10,000	10,000–50,000	Over 50,000	Classes Grouped[b]
Mining	− 1.9	−63.7	− 8.7	− 3.3	− 2.3	− 3.7	− 1.3	− 1.7	− 5.1	− 1.9	—
Total manufacturing	− 2.2	− 6.4	− 4.1	− 4.6	− 5.5	− 5.1	− 4.4	− 4.3	− 4.0	0.6	—
Food	− 1.7	1.5	1.7	0.2	0.8	1.4	1.4	− 4.3	5.6	3.9	—
Tobacco	− 1.8	− 8.7	− 2.8	− 2.0	− 3.1	− 7.3	− 1.4	b	b	b	− 1.5
Textiles	− 5.2	−11.3	− 8.0	− 6.7	− 6.6	− 6.3	− 4.0	− 7.0	b	b	− 4.2
Leather	− 9.2	−19.3	−12.2	− 7.7	−11.9	−10.1	− 8.1	− 9.3	− 7.2	b	—
Rubber	− 0.4	− 4.1	1.9	− 6.5	− 1.5	− 2.8	2.1	− 2.7	− 6.8	—	− 0.4
Forest products	− 6.7	−30.8	−15.7	−11.2	−12.6	− 8.9	− 6.1	− 4.7	− 5.2	1.0	—
Paper	− 0.5	1.9	2.5	1.6	0.8	0.3	− 1.9	0.3	− 0.3	− 1.7	—
Printing	0.9	14.3	5.6	3.4	2.9	2.4	0.2	− 0.7	− 4.0	− 0.6	—
Chemicals	− 2.1	− 7.6	− 1.3	− 2.1	− 2.0	− 1.2	0.2	− 2.6	− 1.9	− 3.0	—
Stone	− 2.1	−12.8	− 4.6	− 4.5	− 5.1	− 4.7	− 3.5	− 3.5	b	b	0.7
Metal	− 3.0	−11.9	− 5.4	− 6.1	− 6.7	− 5.3	− 6.2	− 3.9	− 4.9	− 0.9	—
Construction	− 0.9	− 3.9	− 1.6	− 1.8	− 4.1	− 3.2	− 0.3	− 1.0	b	b	0.3
Transportation and other public utilities	− 0.1	16.1	4.8	1.8	− 3.9	−14.5	− 3.3	− 3.6	− 1.1	0.1	—
Trade	− 4.7	− 6.2	− 3.9	− 5.1	− 5.5	− 5.4	− 5.9	− 4.4	− 2.9	− 1.9	—
Service	− 5.4	2.5	−11.5	0.3	− 1.8	− 3.4	− 6.1	− 6.6	− 6.9	− 7.3	—
Finance	− 3.9	−36.2	− 8.3	− 7.8	− 5.8	− 6.2	− 5.2	− 7.9	− 4.3	0.3	—
All corporations	− 2.3	−10.2	− 5.2	− 5.0	− 5.1	− 5.5	− 4.4	− 5.1	− 3.4	0.3	—

a. Same as footnote a, Table 41.   b. Same as footnote b, Table 41.

Appendix E

ADJUSTED RATIO OF TOTAL PROFIT TO
TOTAL CAPITALIZATION

TABLE 44 shows the effect of adjusting the ratio of total profit to total capitalization by restoring officers' compensation, depreciation and depletion to total profit.[1]

The trends in Table 44 correspond, with some exceptions, to those in Table 13, as far as profitable corporations are concerned, and as far as unprofitable corporations are concerned in 1931 and 1932. However, the trends of the two ratios show little resemblance for the latter group in 1933 and for the group of profitable and unprofitable corporations combined in any of the three years. The adjusted ratios produce more favorable results than the unadjusted ratios in all years in each assets class in each group.

Variations Among Industries

The variations among industrial groups with sub-groups can be seen in Table 45, which is presented without analysis.

---

1. Total profit, it should be remembered, is the sum of the net income and the interest paid; total capitalization is the sum of the net worth, the bonded debt and mortgages, and the notes and accounts payable.

TABLE 44

RATIO OF TOTAL PROFIT PLUS COMPENSATION OF OFFICERS PLUS DEPRECIATION AND DEPLETION, TO TOTAL CAPITALIZATION, BY ASSETS CLASSES, 1931, 1932 AND 1933[a]

(Money Figures and Total Assets Classes in Thousands of Dollars; Ratios in Percentages)

Total Assets Classes	Year	All Returns			Returns Showing Net Income			Returns Showing No Net Income		
		Total Capitalization (A)	Total Profit Plus Compensation of Officers Plus Depreciation and Depletion (B)	Ratio ($\frac{B}{A}$)	Total Capitalization (A)	Total Profit Plus Compensation of Officers Plus Depreciation and Depletion (B)	Ratio ($\frac{B}{A}$)	Total Capitalization (A)	Total Profit Plus Compensation of Officers Plus Depreciation and Depletion[b] (B)	Ratio ($\frac{B}{A}$)
Under 50	1931	3,441,195	291,301	8.5	1,316,065	355,846	27.0	2,125,130	− 64,542	−3.0
	1932	3,520,081	62,009	1.8	639,601	157,145	24.6	2,880,482	− 95,137	−3.3
	1933	3,514,176	278,460	7.9	935,070	252,724	27.0	2,579,103	25,736	1.0
50–100	1931	4,050,931	281,408	7.0	1,602,174	294,393	18.4	2,448,757	− 12,986	−0.5
	1932	3,876,205	93,194	2.4	776,081	129,167	16.6	3,100,124	− 35,972	−1.2
	1933	3,631,067	257,377	7.1	1,110,090	201,620	18.2	2,520,978	55,757	2.2
100–250	1931	8,813,834	460,248	5.2	3,526,850	513,074	14.6	5,286,984	− 52,826	−1.0
	1932	8,204,551	179,210	2.2	1,774,858	244,257	13.8	6,429,693	− 65,046	−1.0
	1933	7,817,954	407,209	5.2	2,489,574	371,729	14.9	5,328,379	35,481	0.7
250–500	1931	9,050,530	402,904	4.5	3,506,946	449,495	12.8	5,543,581	− 46,590	−0.8
	1932	8,297,456	161,067	1.9	1,946,646	232,375	11.9	6,350,809	− 71,305	−1.1
	1933	7,792,866	344,667	4.4	2,607,093	336,931	12.9	5,185,773	7,735	0.2
500–1,000	1931	10,592,606	395,729	3.7	3,901,015	446,723	11.5	6,691,590	− 50,994	−0.8
	1932	9,676,781	147,720	1.5	2,351,339	249,334	10.6	7,325,441	−101,615	−1.4
	1933	9,160,056	373,122	4.1	3,166,426	368,212	11.6	5,993,631	4,910	0.1

194

TABLE 44 (Continued)

Total Assets Classes	Year	All Returns			Returns Showing Net Income			Returns Showing No Net Income		
		Total Capitalization (A)	Total Profit Plus Compensation of Officers Plus Depreciation and Depletion (B)	Ratio $\frac{B}{A}$	Total Capitalization (A)	Total Profit Plus Compensation of Officers Plus Depreciation and Depletion (B)	Ratio $\frac{B}{A}$	Total Capitalization (A)	Total Profit Plus Compensation of Officers Plus Depreciation and Depletion[b] (B)	Ratio $\frac{B}{A}$
1,000–5,000	1931	28,101,872	857,624	3.1	9,873,795	1,003,011	10.2	18,228,079	−145,386	−0.8
	1932	25,952,670	388,744	1.5	6,495,583	570,804	8.8	19,457,088	−182,061	−0.9
	1933	24,598,623	801,131	3.3	8,574,774	846,067	9.9	16,023,849	− 44,936	−0.3
5,000–10,000	1931	13,099,730	430,591	3.3	4,736,310	467,077	9.9	8,363,421	− 36,486	−0.4
	1932	12,663,479	186,865	1.5	3,640,253	307,356	8.4	9,023,226	−120,490	−1.3
	1933	12,114,823	353,911	2.9	4,500,343	404,795	9.0	7,614,480	− 50,884	−0.7
10,000–50,000	1931	31,306,391	1,266,435	4.1	12,796,769	1,214,863	9.5	18,509,622	51,573	0.3
	1932	29,129,290	659,818	2.3	9,084,977	732,205	8.1	20,044,313	− 72,387	−0.4
	1933	28,297,027	965,377	3.4	11,628,052	1,018,874	8.8	16,668,974	− 53,497	−0.3
50,000 and over	1931	106,158,158	5,869,904	5.5	43,603,273	3,876,705	8.9	62,554,884	1,993,200	3.2
	1932	100,120,693	4,164,580	4.2	32,106,654	2,475,211	7.7	68,014,039	1,689,369	2.5
	1933	95,895,465	4,132,553	4.3	38,060,085	2,633,020	6.9	57,835,381	1,499,534	2.6
All corporations	1931	214,615,247	10,256,142	4.8	84,863,199	8,621,183	10.2	129,752,051	1,634,961	1.3
	1932	201,441,203	6,043,209	3.0	58,815,989	5,097,852	8.7	142,625,214	945,359	0.7
	1933	192,822,057	7,913,805	4.1	73,071,507	6,433,972	8.8	119,750,548	1,479,833	1.2

a. Computed from *Statistics of Income*, page references same as for Table 2.　　b. Minus signs indicate deficits.

TABLE 45

RATIO OF TOTAL PROFIT PLUS COMPENSATION OF OFFICERS PLUS DEPRECIATION AND DEPLETION, TO TOTAL CAPITALIZATION, BY INDUSTRIAL GROUPS AND BY ASSETS CLASSES, 1932: ALL CORPORATIONS[a]

(Total Assets Classes in Thousands of Dollars; Ratios in Percentages)

Industrial Groups	Total	Total Assets Classes									
		Under 50	50–100	100–250	250–500	500–1,000	1,000–5,000	5,000–10,000	10,000–50,000	Over 50,000	Classes Grouped[b]
Mining	2.1	– 3.1	2.8	4.1	4.6	2.4	2.6	2.3	2.7	1.2	—
Total manufacturing	2.5	3.0	3.2	2.3	1.5	1.3	0.7	1.5	0.9	4.0	—
Food	5.9	8.1	8.1	6.6	6.6	6.3	4.9	4.4	3.2	8.0	—
Tobacco	12.5	4.5	6.1	7.9	5.3	0.7	6.3	b	b	8.8	16.3
Textiles	0.3	2.4	2.2	2.0	1.8	0.4	0.6	– 2.0	b	b	– 0.5
Leather	0.2	– 2.3	2.1	3.2	– 2.4	– 2.8	– 1.6	2.7	b	b	4.4
Rubber	2.3	6.7	7.7	1.9	4.3	– 0.8	4.2	–	b	b	2.2
Forest products	– 2.6	– 9.6	– 5.1	– 4.5	– 6.5	– 3.7	b	b	– 3.1	– 2.1	– 0.1
Paper	3.1	6.5	8.3	6.7	5.4	5.5	2.9	4.3	b	b	2.3
Printing	5.3	13.2	8.5	8.5	8.3	6.6	5.5	8.4	b	b	2.7
Chemicals	5.9	4.2	6.2	5.9	6.5	6.6	7.6	7.4	4.7	8.5	—
Stone	1.1	– 3.6	0.4	0.4	0.9	0.2	0.2	0.2	b	b	2.6
Metal	– 0.7	– 2.1	0.4	– 1.0	– 1.4	– 1.3	– 2.9	– 1.1	– 2.0	0.4	—
Construction	4.6	3.7	4.6	4.1	4.0	2.7	4.6	b	b	b	6.1
Transportation and other public utilities	4.4	1.4	9.8	8.4	5.8	2.8	4.8	4.0	5.0	4.3	—
Trade	2.0	2.3	2.3	1.3	– 0.7	0.8	0.5	2.0	2.9	4.7	—
Service	0.8	6.2	0.3	3.2	2.2	1.9	0.8	1.0	b	b	—
Finance	2.2	– 5.8	1.1	1.4	1.9	1.4	1.4	0.1	1.8	5.0	– 1.3
All corporations	3.0	1.8	2.4	2.2	1.9	1.5	1.5	1.5	2.3	4.2	—

a. Same as footnote a, Table 41. b. Same as footnote b, Table 41.

GLOSSARY

GLOSSARY

(Only those important terms are defined which might otherwise be subject to misinterpretation. The following definitions give the meanings as commonly applied to these terms in the text. Where other meanings are intended, statements to that effect are given in the text or in footnotes.)

All corporations. The combination of the profitable and unprofitable corporations of any group or class under discussion. "All corporations" has the same meaning as "all returns," the term used in *Statistics of Income.* Data on all returns from that source embrace only the active corporations submitting balance sheets to the Bureau of Internal Revenue, unless otherwise specified.

Assets. Total assets, i.e., all assets listed in corporate balance sheets.

Capital assets. Lands, buildings and equipment, less depreciation.

Capital funds. As used in Chapter 9, represent aggregate book value of common and preferred capital stock, surplus, undivided profits, reserves for contingencies, retirement fund for preferred stock, and reserve for dividend payable in common stock.

Capitalization. The par value of all stocks and bonds.

Deficit. The excess of total costs over gross income.

Dividends. Cash payments only. Unless otherwise specified same as "total dividends."

Earning assets. As used in Chapter 9, same as loans and investments, but includes any other assets from which income was derived.

Earnings. A term used in the general sense of profits.

Fixed debt. Bonded debt and mortgages.

Floating debt. Notes and accounts payable, as distinguished from bonds and mortgages.

Giant corporations or class. Corporations with assets of at least $50 million each.

Gross earnings. As used in Chapter 9, represents total earnings from current operations.

Gross income. Total receipts in all forms and from all sources, including net profit from sale of capital assets but not gross receipts from these items. Gross income has the same meaning as "total compiled receipts," the term used in *Statistics of Income.*

Loans and investments. Loans, discounts, overdrafts, and all bonds, stocks and securities.

Loss. Same as deficit.

Losses. As used in Chapter 9, losses on loans, bonds, stocks and other assets, and depreciation on banking-house furniture and fixtures.

Net earnings. As used in Chapter 9, gross earnings less current operating expenses.

Net income. The excess of gross income over total costs. When a minus sign appears before a net income figure or net income ratio it indicates that there was a deficit or loss, instead of a net income. Strictly speaking, net income is the profit before allowance for Federal income and excess profits taxes, but throughout the text these taxes have been deducted from net income proper, and net income, therefore, means the amount available for dividends. Net income has the same meaning as "compiled net profit less income tax," the term used in *Statistics of Income.*

Net profit. As used in Chapter 11 only, this term means the amount available to meet fixed charges.

Net profits, or net addition to profits. As used in Chapter 9, represent net earnings plus other income or less other losses. If losses exceed net earnings the result is a deficit.

Net worth. The sum of all issues of preferred and common stocks, plus the surplus and undivided profits.

Officers' compensation. Salaries plus other payments made to corporate officers.

Other income. As used in Chapter 9, earnings due to recoveries on loans, bonds, stocks and other assets written off, and profits on securities sold.

Profit. Same as net income, but see "net profit" and "total profit."

Profitable corporations. Corporations whose gross income exceeds their total costs. "Profitable corporations" has the same meaning as "returns showing net income," the term used in *Statistics of Income.*

Size. Except when otherwise stated the size of corporations is measured in terms of the book value of their total assets. The size of banks is measured in Chapter 9 by the book value of their combined loans and investments.

Statutory net income. Total net income less dividends from domestic corporations and interest on tax-exempt obligations.

Stockholders' equity. Same as net worth.

Total capitalization. Net worth plus bonded debt and mortgages. When used in connection with data published in *Statistics of Income,* total capitalization also includes notes and accounts payable.

Total costs. Total expenses of all kinds whether representing actual payments (or obligations to pay) or merely bookkeeping items such as bad debts, depreciation and depletion. Losses on sale of capital assets are included, as are all taxes other than Federal income and excess profits taxes. Total costs has the same meaning as "total statutory deductions," the term used in *Statistics of Income.*

Total dividends. Cash dividends paid on preferred and common stock issues combined.

Total profit. Net income plus interest paid on borrowed capital.

Turnover. As used in Chapter 7, the ratio of gross income to either net worth or total capitalization.

Unprofitable corporations. Corporations whose total costs exceed their gross income. "Unprofitable corporations" has the same meaning as "returns showing no net income," the term used in *Statistics of Income.*

Water. In capital structure, "water" represents the difference between the book value of the assets and their "real" or "true" value.